PRISMS

Reflections on This Journey We Call Life

By James Hollis, PHD

CHIRON PUBLICATIONS • ASHEVILLE, NORTH CAROLINA

www.ChironPublications.com

Interior and cover design by Danijela Mijailovic
Printed primarily in the United States of America.

ISBN 978-1-63051-929-2 paperback
ISBN 978-1-63051-930-8 hardcover
ISBN 978-1-63051-931-5 electronic
ISBN 978-1-63051-932-2 limited edition paperback

Library of Congress Cataloging-in-Publication Data

Names: Hollis, James, 1940- author.
Title: Prisms : reflections on this journey we call life / by James Hollis, PHD.
Description: Asheville, North Carolina : Chiron Publications, 2021. | Includes bibliographical references. | Summary: "Prisms: Reflections on the Journey We Call Life summarizes a lifetime of observing, engaging, and exploring why we are here, in service to what, and what life asks of us. These eleven essays, all written recently, examine how we understand ourselves, and often we have to reframe that understanding, the nature and gift of comedy, the imagination, desire, as well as our encounters with narcissism, and aging. James Hollis, Ph.D., a Jungian Analyst in Washington, D.C., explores the roadblocks we encounter and our on-going challenge to live our brief journey with as much courage, insight, and resolve as we can bring to the table"— Provided by publisher.
Identifiers: LCCN 2021010159 (print) | LCCN 2021010160 (ebook) | ISBN 9781630519292 (paperback) | ISBN 9781630519308 (hard-cover) | ISBN 9781630519315 (electronic) | ISBN 9781630519322 (limited edition paperback)
Subjects: LCSH: Self-actualization (Psychology) | Jungian psychology. | Adulthood.
Classification: LCC BF637.S4 H5945 2021 (print) | LCC BF637.S4 (ebook) | DDC 158.1—dc23
LC record available at https://lccn.loc.gov/2021010159
LC ebook record available at https://lccn.loc.gov/2021010160

Books by James Hollis

- *Harold Pinter: The Poetics of Silence*
- *The Middle Passage: From Misery to Meaning at Midlife*
- *Under Saturn's Shadow: The Wounding and Healing of Men*
- *Tracking the Gods: The Place of Myth in Modern Life*
- *Swamplands of the Soul: New Life from Dismal Places*
- *The Eden Project: In Search of the Magical Other*
- *The Archetypal Imagination*
- *Creating a Life: Finding Your Individual Path*
- *On This Journey We Call our Life*
- *Mythologems: Incarnations of the Invisible World*
- *Finding Meaning in the Second Half of Life*
- *Why Good People Do Bad Things: Exploring Our Darker Selves*
- *What Matters Most: Living a More Considered Life*
- *Hauntings: Dispelling the Ghosts that Run Our Lives*
- *Living the Examined Life: Wisdom for the Second Half of the Journey*
- *Living Between Worlds: Finding Personal Resilience in Changing Times*

Table of Contents

Permissions

I thank the following publishers for their permission to reprint these essays: "Permutations of Desire," *Parabola*, Vol. 35, No. 3.

"All Is Fire: The Imagination as Aperture into Psyche," *The Unconscious Roots of Creativity*, Kathryn Madden, Ed. Chiron Publications.

"Narcissism's Forlorn Hope," *A Clear and Present Danger: Narcissism in the Era of Donald Trump*, Eds. Leonard Cruz and Steven Buser, Chiron Publications.

"Theogonys and Therapies: A Jungian Perspective on Evil," *Humanity's Dark Side: Evil, Destructive Experience, and Psychotherapy*. Eds. Arthur C. Bohart, *et al*. American Psychological Association.

"*The Rag and Bone Shop of the Heart: Yeats's Passage from* Puer Aeternus *to Wise Old Man*," Ed. Nancy Cater, Spring Publications.

"For Every Tatter in Our Mortal Dress: Stayin' Alive at the Front of the Mortal Parade," *C. G. Jung and Aging: Possibilities and Potentials for the Second Half of Life*, Eds. Leslie Sawin, Lionel Corbett, Michael Carbine. Spring Publications.

This book is dedicated to

My Jill,
And our children:
Taryn and Tim, Jonah and Seah
The people of the
Jung Society of Washington
and
With great thanks to
Steve Buser
Len Cruz
Jennifer Fitzgerald

Preface

"Just so it's clear—
No whining on the journey.
If you whine, you'll get stuck
Somewhere with people
Like yourself."
                Stephen Dunn, "Before We Leave"

I keep thinking I could be, perhaps should be, a normal person and just turn on the telly and watch sports when not working at my day job as a therapist. (My team of choice is the Philadelphia Eagles, if you need to know. So for that reason, Dallas and New York fans will not get this book and should stop reading now). Unfortunately, the *Daimon,* apparently my *Daimon,* seems to have other ideas. It's rather like being a serial killer. I have normal desires, walk and talk normally, and then some sinister force takes over.

What is a *Daimon,* you ask. It is a tutelary spirit, a directive intermediary between the gods and humans. It is not a god and not a demon. It is an autonomous Hermetic link between higher and lower powers. (Hermes was the "messenger" of the gods; his Latin form became Mercury, the logo for Western Union). Plato said that Socrates did not speak; the Daimon spoke *through* him, using him for that purpose. And so too the artist who paints or composes. The Daimon directs the hand, provides the compelling energy. The human has only one choice—whether or not to submit to the Daimon.

The Daimon speaks to all of us in various ways although we often resist its urgent presence. Most of us, most of the time, find ways to slip-slide away from its invasive summons. Sometimes this avoidance leads to a quiet, untroubled life, but perhaps it also leads to a diminished journey, and sometimes it even pathologizes. As Jung once said, a neurosis is a repressed or a neglected god. So it is, I think, with the Daimon.

When I was a young adult, I dutifully wrote a dissertation on the tension of opposites as manifested in the life and work of the poet W. B. Yeats. Shortly after that, I wrote the first book in America on the relatively unknown British playwright Harold Pinter—all this before age 30. To be employed in academia, I had to demonstrate that I could. And then I stopped for decades. As an academic, I was supposed to publish or perish. But something inside protested, and I dried up for two and a half decades. If I wanted to write under assignment, I would be a journalist or a copy writer for an advertising firm—both honorable professions, no doubt. But that internal resistance was compelling and apparently was asking something more from me than promotion or a small raise in salary.

I was a professor of humanities at private and state universities, and then from 1977-82, seeking, driven perhaps, to go deeper than the life of the conscious mind, entered Jungian analytic training at the Mother Ship in Zürich, the *Jung-Institut*. Upon returning, I started speaking and teaching in Philadelphia, which then spread to Wilmington, and then Ottawa, and then Atlanta, Portland, Seattle, Vancouver, and Montreal, and soon everywhere, most commonly at Jung societies. Then, unexpectedly, the Daimon arrived, pushed up through the floorboards of the adaptive self, and started hounding me. From that came 16 more books, plus a thesis in Zürich that became a book, and it hasn't let go of me yet. Often, I want to say, "Stop, already!" But it persists.

So, I see this book as "late" essays, given that all were written lately and given that I am 80 and dealing with at least two cancers. Since cancer took out the entire female side of my ancestors, I should say "final," but I also know better not to predict anymore. The gods apparently laugh at such inflation and send the Daimon on its intrusive mission once again.

The reason I am spending the reader's time on this subject, clearly the stuff of someone else's life, and not necessarily the reader's, is that possibly I have learned something here that might be of to help the reader. But do continue warned. I said I resisted the external demands to publish in order to prove my competence, to get minuscule raises, promotion, a better office. And I am glad I did. But in the end I could not resist the insurgent demands of the Daimon within.

In the first half of life, our summons is to build an ego strong enough to enter the world, deal with it, meet its demands, and create a living space for ourselves in it. This is seemingly what growing up requires and all life apparently expects. But if we are privileged to live longer than that, we often find other, insistent demands beginning to wash up on our shores from the vast sea within. While I refused to submit to academia, I could not in the end refuse to submit to the Daimon. In fact, I think the meaning of the entire second half of life, (second half used more metaphorically than chronologically) is about finding, or submitting to, something larger than our ego needs, something larger than our complexes with their insistent chatter.

If the first half of life is about *"what does the world want from me, and how do I meet its demands,"* the second "half" is about *"what wants to enter the world through me?"* I believe I have been privileged, compelled perhaps, to know the answer to that personal question and have been living it in various ways for the last decades. I further believe that we all swim in mystery, and that that mystery—what some call the voice of God, some the Daimon, some "destiny"—seeks its expression *through* us. We are the humble vehicles of that expression. It little matters if we wish that summons—it happens. And the more we submit, the richer our life becomes because we are flush with some kind of energy, and we experience our lives, however conflictual and traumatic, as meaningful. The experience of enduring meaning is not found in the precincts of pleasure, affluence, or achievement, as we once thought evident, but in surrendering to something developmental, redeeming, and enlarging, something coursing through us, something wishing embodiment *through* us.

Submission to something larger than our ego worldview and its agenda does not sound attractive to most folks. The ego is typically a nascent tyrant and, while delusional, believes that what it knows is sufficient, that it is in charge, and that it is making proper choices. Both an honest review of our history and frequently suffering an insurgent psycho-pathology as an expression of revolt inside tell us otherwise. But ego persists in its inflationary march. Thus, I have come to agree with those many religious thinkers and mystics who for so many millennia concluded that if we do not submit to something larger, we will inadvertently submit to something quite smaller, and thus prove unworthy to have been in-carnated into history.

As I mentioned, I am in the middle of treatment for two cancers as I write this book, as well as sequestering from the pandemic. I describe my attitude toward these unwanted restrictions as "militant submission." Though the prognosis is good, a long road of submission to treatment lies ahead, as so many others have experienced. Having long accepted the fact that I am not exempt from mortality and having accepted that I now have to be a captive of a medical regimen, I plan to keep as active and grow as much as I can under the circumstances. I want to continue to live fully for many reasons—to be here for my Jill and others who may need me, and to keep learning because life gets more and more interesting. (Plus, any year we beat Dallas is a year worth attending). But I am also ready to depart, knowing I have had the privilege of an interesting and extended life not granted to most of humanity. So, what is there to complain about?

As a child, I considered my teachers—and I can name them all still, along with Esther Hunn, local librarian—my heroes because they introduced me to a larger world out there.

I saw my father sacrifice his life in the factory and shoveling coal for us. I saw my mother sacrifice her life working as a secretary. Both were honorable, and both so riven and oppressed by anxiety, so constricted by poverty and lack of education, and so forlorn of permission or hope for something more, that my teachers helped fill the gap by seeing something in me and making helpful suggestions along the way.

Many years later, while writing my book on the wounding and healing of men, I found my old college football coach and wrote to him. He was still alive and living in Indianapolis. He was kind enough to write back to me in pencil: "Good to hear from you, Jimmy. We remember those days: you get knocked down, you get up, buckle your helmet, and get ready for the next play." That was it, that was all, but it was a lesson of a lifetime. So, why would I not also devote my life to education? And thus, I have been teaching for nearly six decades now. In addition to university posts, I have traveled over a million and a half air miles to speak, most often to Jungian societies. (After all those liftoffs and touchdowns, and knowing the physics of flight, I still can't believe that something weighing hundreds of thousands of pounds of aluminum, gas, plus all those little peanut bags, can really get off the ground and stay there). Some topics, such as "The Middle Passage," "The Eden Project," "Finding Meaning in the Second Half of Life," were presented over 60 times to different groups. I never tired of repeating the subject because the audience was always different, and I was becoming different through our interaction. (As Jung noted, all relationships are alchemical, changing both parties, whether they know it or not).

As an introvert, such public speaking is an unnatural act, but I soon learned to remind myself that the good folks in those venues were not there because of me but because they were hungering for tools and ideas that would help them in their lives. If I thought that Jung's analytic psychology was helpful to me, why would I not want to share that with others, as my teachers did for me? In sum, I am filled with gratitude for all of them and for the opportunity to live in a moment in history when a constricted child could find a way toward possible futures.

Among my clients over 65, most have dreams that review their lives, seeking perhaps to discern the threads, the continuities, the old wounds—how they were understood then and how they are understood now. What did those events, personalities, historic fortuities make one do or keep one from doing? And what remains to be addressed—not only in unfinished business but in the continuing summons to growth and development?

In the autonomous, and ineluctable, motions of the psyche, we are continuously pulled into an unfolding future. Our egos, usually under the influence of one complex or another, generally walk down the street backward and are continuously shocked when they fall into a hole of some kind. The human psyche is terribly conservative much of the time. It wishes to keep the *status quo ante* as long as it can, even when the world around it has changed. It is a fool thing to do, but we all do it. As I wrote one client, frozen with fear, "Nothing will change until you decide that fear is a poor star to steer your ship by. Whatever you have to face is never as bad as living a fugitive life. What you have to face is perhaps scary to the child but only troubling to the adult." It is true that Satchel Paige said, "Never trouble till trouble troubles you," but the adult has to take over sooner or later, or that child never has someone like the adult us standing by to protect him. As Congressman John Lewis said, find "good trouble" and engage it. Zorba the Greek added, "Sometimes you have to take your belt off and go looking for trouble."

So, while our most constructive attitude is in service to growth and development, the paradox is that such development may also oblige militant surrender—surrender not only to aging and health issues, and the vicissitudes of the outer world, but surrender to what wishes to carry us to a different place. A friend and colleague recently dreamed that she was on a raft on the open seas, and a large form emerged from the depths, and she found herself poised over a beluga whale, which carries her and her craft: "As it moves under me, I roll with it knowing somewhere inside that I have to ride the momentum, knowing it is the whale, not I, who is in charge. It is a marvelous ride, and I smile as it then swims away."

Don't we all want to know more about those large forms that roll beneath the surface of our lives? Don't we all want to experience the full joy and terror of that ride? Don't we all want to engage what carries us through this journey we call our life?

So, the reader can see, and even I can see, why living a normal life and watching the ballgame is pretty much out the window, for now.

James Hollis,
Washington, DC
2020

Chapter One
Archetypal Presences: The Large Forms Rolling Beneath the Surface of Our Lives

> ...*the light sings eternal*
> *a pale flare over marshes*
> *where the salt hay whispers*
> *to tide's changes.*
>
> Ezra Pound, *The Cantos*

Ezra Pound's lines evoke the paradox that we, fleeting beings in fleeting moments on a speck of dust in oceans of dark space, *also* embody something that persists. What light sings eternal, what persists amid the sea-salt tidal changes? Let us consider how archetypal energies flow through our species, and out of the roiling chaos of atoms create a world we can know and provide us something timeless amid our short and troubled transits.

In his memoir, *Memories, Dreams, Reflections*, Carl Jung surveys his life in an oral recollection. It is, he noted to his reader, not an account of the events of his life—that is mere biography—but an unfolding of the psycho-spiritual way stations on his long journey of discovery. Similarly, a number of my clients are over 65, and we have noted that many of their dreams are seeming reviews of their lives. It may be that the psyche continues to sort and sift through the accumulated debris of our histories, and keeps inquiring: What was that about? what was the reason, or meaning, for that? What stood at the railway switch of life and sent the train of consequences down this line versus another? What has this whole journey been about? If it is true, that the client's psyche is not just reminiscing, then is it possible that the psyche, this meaning-making, meaning-needing organ we all possess, is still trying to work it all out, give us a view that transcends our daily enmeshment in the details, the detritus of moments that pass so quickly? Even when life provides us only with shards, glimmers, glimpses, don't we all want to see *the bigger picture*?

When we come to our end, if we are conscious, will we not wonder what our journey was about? Will we perseverate over the mistakes, the roads not taken, the woundings? Or will we remain curious, tracing what was unfolding from within us all that while? While we may grieve the imminent loss of this world, might we remember the words of Rainer Maria Rilke to a young poet:

> *{do} not be frightened if a sadness rises up*
> *before you larger than any you have ever seen; if a*
> *restiveness, like light and cloud shadows, passes*
> *over your hands and over all you do. You must think*
> *that something is happening with you, that life has*
> *not forgotten you, that it holds you in its hand; it*
> *will not let you fall. Why do you want to shut out of*
> *your life any uneasiness, any miseries, or any*
> *depressions? For after all, you do not know what*
> *work these conditions are doing inside you.*[1]

---

[1] R. M. Rilke, *Letters to a Young Poet.*
https://www.goodreads.com/quotes/805078-we-have-no-reason-to-mistrust-our-world-for-it

Or will we instead, in a moment of cynicism, think of this whirl and wonder of life a bizarre, delusional fiction, a brief part in a larger drama than we can fathom, and perhaps conclude that we played the most trivial of roles? Were we real? Were we really here? Were we something more than a fictional character? Danusha Lemeris wonders this about fictional characters, and the various fictions we may be serving in her poem of the same title:

Fictional Characters

Do they ever want to escape?
Climb out of the white pages
and enter our world?

Holden Caulfield slipping in the movie theater
to catch the two o'clock
Anna Karenina sitting in a diner,
reading the paper as the waitress
serves up a cheeseburger.

Even Hector, on break from the Iliad,
takes a stroll through the park,
admires the tulips.

Maybe they grew tired
of the author's mind,
all its twists and turns.

Or were finally weary
of stumbling around Pamplona,

a bottle in each fist,
eating lotuses on the banks of the Nile.

For others, it was just too hot
in the small California town
where they'd been written into
a lifetime of plowing fields.

Whatever the reason,
here they are, roaming the city streets
rain falling on their phantasmal shoulders.

Wouldn't you, if you could?
Step out of your own story,
to lean against a doorway
of the Five & Dime, sipping your coffee,

your life, somewhere far behind you,
all its heat and toil nothing but a tale
resting in the hands of a stranger,
the sidewalk ahead wet and glistening.[2]

So, when Jung dictated the following paragraph in his *Memories, Dreams, Reflections*, I took note of something peculiar in his suggestion of multiple intrapsychic characters in a large, archetypal drama. We think we have generated what transpires for us, but is not that the delusion of the ego

---

[2] https://www.thesunmagazine.org/issues/407/fictional-characters by Danusha Laméris from *The Moons of August*. © Autumn House Press, 2014.

consciousness that prides itself on its sovereignty, its sui generis identity, its autonomy? And is not that attitude like the flea that bestrides the crest of a lion and imagines that all other beasts are afraid of his magnificence?

The human ego is a thin wafer floating on an iridescent ocean. It can so easily be engulfed by the billows around it, but it arrogates to itself a privileged position, fancies itself a sovereign in a world of lesser beings, and makes large choices having large consequences. But how often is it really in charge? Is the human ego ever really free of other influences; is it not often captive to dissociative clusters of energy known as *complexes* and an unwitting servant to their archaic types? Is it not carried by large archetypal winds across the turning pages of ragged time?

While the ego consciousness that we all prize so highly serves a concrete purpose, namely, making decisions that help us navigate the perils and promises of daily life, it is also subject to forces it cannot know. After all, the general problematic of the unconscious is that it is unconscious. So, that the sorting and sifting of influences, choice, consequence, and all their sequelae that I perceive among my older analysands, is how the psyche itself is informing, perhaps teaching, perhaps correcting the ego's brief reign as a presumptive sovereign.

But let us hear Jung's paragraph first:

Philemon and other figures of my fantasies brought home to me the crucial insight that there are things in the psyche which I do not produce, but which produce themselves and have their own life. Philemon represented a force which was not myself. In my fantasies I held conversations with him, and he said things which I had not consciously thought. For I observed clearly that it was he who spoke, not I. He said I treated thoughts as if I generated them myself, but in his view thoughts were like animals in the forest, or people in a room, or birds in the air, and added, "If you should see people in a room, you would not think that you had made those people, or that you were responsible for them." It was he who taught me psychic objectivity, the reality of the psyche. Through him the distinction was clarified between myself and the object of my thought. He confronted me in an objective manner, and I understood that there is something in me which can say things that I do not know and do not intend, things which may even be directed against me.[3]

Let's unpack this paragraph for a moment. When confronted, as many of us have been, with an insurgency from within at midlife, Jung decided not to down an analgesic pill or seek a guru through whom he might find an authority to offer him clarity and direction. Instead, he chose to turn within, to pay attention to the thoughts, feelings, images that flooded him from below, and to record them or paint them. In seeking to identify and record these affective invasions, he

[3] C. G. Jung. *Memories, Dreams, Reflections.* New York: Pantheon Press, 1961. https://www.goodreads.com/quotes/309513-philemon-and-other-figures-of-my-fantasies-brought-home-to

both honored their authority but also rendered them sufficiently conscious as to open to him an aperture into understanding why they had come. Perhaps he was forced, as we all may be by the appearance of an unwanted depression, a disturbing dream, or a collapse of our psychological frames, to admit the autonomy of the unconscious, the otherness of the *Other*. In "naming" the *Other*, he gave it a respect while also objectifying it sufficiently as to allow him to dialogue with it. Only dialogue—what he called in Swiss German, the *Auseinandersetzung*, setting conscious ego life over against the "consciousness" of the *Other* that was hitherto unconscious— enlarges.

Accordingly, *Philemon* was the name he gave, or which presented itself to him, for the numinous personification of ancient wisdom who seemed to be directing this storm of affect-laden imagery that flooded him. Reportedly, he is "told" by Philemon and others that he has not imagined them, but that they exist in some way as objectively "other" in that they confront the ego in its limitations. In admitting the autonomy of the other, Jung begins to realize the objective reality of matters psychic. By *psychic* I mean, those internal agencies confronting our sensibility in some autonomous and felt way. When, for example, we fall into a complex, we have our sense of self and world changed, are momentarily "possessed" by somatic manifestations in our bodies, driven by affect that stirs us, and often unwillingly serve reflexive enactments of the splinter program that history generated. In those moments we are in a subjective experience of the other as objective *other*. At its worst, this is the stuff of psychosis, where one communes with demons, daimons, and deities that overwhelm the fragile ego state; but Jung held to his conscious standpoint at the same time and never forgot his grounding in *this* world, as his vast scholarship, his practice, and his social life demonstrated. Though he wrote, Philemon spoke, "not I," he experienced Philemon as that other who confronted him, but he never lost contact with the *I* which stayed grounded in this world.

That other reminded him that if he saw animals in the forest or people in the room, that he had not created them but that they had come to him as *Other*. And, when that other becomes part of us, we are summoned to take in their being, their testimony. So, we grow from all our relationships with others, without forgetting that we are separate from our friends or partners.

Because this Other is *other*, it is not necessarily the friend of ego comfort or predictability. The summons of that Other is often intimidating, even frightening to the ego world, such as when we are called to grow or sacrifice something dear to our hearts. But, presumably, this Other carries the imperative and the agendas of nature, or divinity, and therefore will be served one way or the other. If we flee that summons, it will spill into the world through projections, or unconscious behaviors, or creep up on us through illness or compelling dreams.

So, whenever possessed by that Other, we risk being disconnected from the reality of the immanent world. In a sustained disconnect, this is called "psychosis." But in a world in which the ego holds its position and is able to record, dialogue with, learn from that Other, the whole is enlarged and emerges less divided and discordant. As Jung writes:

16

"At times I feel as if I am spread out over the landscape and inside things, and am myself living in every tree, in the plashing of the waves, in the clouds and the animals that come and go, in the procession of the seasons. There is nothing in the Tower that has not grown into its own form over the decades, nothing with which I am not linked. Here everything has its history, and mine: here is space for the spaceless kingdom of the world's and the psyche's hinterland."[4]

* * * *

While complexes are personal and reflect our unique biographies, the archetypes are transpersonal and link us to all of humanity and serve as both template and umbilical bloodweb into the substrata of nature itself. It would help us to think of an archetype as a *verb* and not a noun because if we carried archetypes as nouns, they would be visible on our MRIs or our CAT scans. They would be objects. In other words, you may know a noun—a person, place or a thing— but if you rather think of them as energies, purposive energies, patterning energies, you begin to appreciate their dynamic character. But energies in service to what? In service, of course, to nature's purpose, not necessarily the ego's. However, it is through *this innate archetypal formative process that we, as individuals, link to the universal and, as time-bound mortals, link to the timeless.* The dream you dream tonight may replicate someone's dream from ancient Babylonia or echo some contemporary's dream from Irkutsk or Samarkand. The

---

[4] Jung, *Ibid.* p. 225.

seeming free behavior of this hour may be driven by a formative energy repeatedly honored through the myths and wisdom literature of the ancients.

Now, I want to read these three sentences from Jung. They're simple sentences, but yet very packed. And I want to break them down a bit. He said, *"The archetypes are the numinous structural elements of the psyche and present a certain autonomy and specific energy which enables them to attract out of the conscious minds, those contents which are best suited to themselves. These symbols act as transformers. Their function being to convert libido or psychic energy from lower to a higher form."*[5]

That's just three sentences, but they are loaded. Let us back up a little bit and look closer. The archetype is *numinous*, meaning we don't choose it, nor does it originate in our conscious life. It is an autonomous energy that's independent of ego consciousness. We can become aware of its impact; we can be driven by it; or we can have it operating in our lives without even having any awareness of its influence.

He also said, "It's a structural element." In other words, it *organizes*. That's why I say it's a *verb*. Maybe life is inherently meaningless. It is only atoms combining and decombining, but what characterizes human experience is that we organize the world into patterns through these instinctually generative interactions with the environment. Out of those patternings arise our sense of structure, meaning, purpose. This is our unique gift to the brute nature of nature naturing.

---

[5] C. G. Jung. *The Collected Works, CW5, Symbols of Transformation*, para. 308.

Jung goes on to say the patterning process attracts out of a conscious mind, *"those contents which are best suited for themselves."* So, in a dream, you may merge your third-grade teacher with a movie character and a family member—all in service to the symbolic field where ordinary ego boundaries dissolve and daytime logic is suspended. The seemingly disparate features of our lives have hidden unities, and a dynamic relationship through that symbolic field.

Perhaps we can summarize this idea this way: *Archetypes are our psychic pictures of the puzzling world into which we were thrown.* They give us a handle on the evanescent forms of things and enable us to stand in relationships to the large Other that the world brings to us.

Let me give an example of how the archetypal imagination works within our species, how it autonomously emerges to address our deepest longing to relate, to understand.

* * * *

I shudder each late autumn as I reflect on the hardships our distant ancestors bore as the sun plummets into the underworld, an annual *catabasis* that must have been, if not terrifying, at best problematic for their survival. Given that we are that animal that desires to know, to develop stories that help us relate to the inexplicable and sometimes monstrous forces around us, their primal, archetypal imagination conjured up all sorts of cosmic animals that had eaten the sun or malevolent gods that had abducted it from its office of warming our crops and our person.

As an example, I think on my visit to Newgrange, about an hour's drive north of Dublin, Eire. A number of years ago, what were thought simply to be hills were revealed to be burial chambers. (Aerial photography is helping find many more such sites). Today, rightly controlled by the government to protect its fragile state, one can go down into the recesses of one of those domes. (From afar, they almost look like football stadia). One descends about 20 meters into a cavern in which one light bulb now hangs. The guide informs that this structure was built circa 5,200 years ago, which makes it older than the pyramids and much older than Stonehenge. When she turns off that one bulb, we know what dark dark is really like. We are, for a while, one with those whose bodies had once been placed there: sojourners in the underworld.

Further, we see what is called a latchkey slot in the ceiling about the size of a shoebox. In the late days of December, for a matter of minutes each dark day, that slot is aligned with the sun, now at its farthest perigee from our sight. Stunningly, the room is briefly illumined by that light. There in the dark cavern, in the darkest time of the year in the Northern Hemisphere, the light exfoliates. What are we to make of that elaborate construction that so clearly was tied to a solstice ("sun standing still") ritual?

Standing in the depths of that sacred space, I had three thoughts, which came to me in this order. First, I marveled at the *engineering* acumen that had cantilevered those stones to create that space. And I hoped that their skill would persist for another few years, given that I and others were under those stones. Second, I was moved by their *astronomical* sophistication, which could so accurately calculate the movement of the stars and planets that they could only dimly see by the naked eye. Thirdly, I realized and was moved by recognizing that I was in the presence of the *Great Mother archetype* of which Jung spoke.

Remember, an archetype is recognized through its incarnation in a form available to consciousness but is not created by individual consciousness. It is a timeless, patterning process whose contents vary greatly, but whose form is universal. The Great Mother is a personification of the forces of the birth, death, rebirth process through which all individuals and cultures move.

So there, in that pre-Celtic cavern, I bore witness to the archetypal idea that even in death, even in the darkest hours, a scintilla of light is present, the germ of rebirth, renewal, whereby the great cycle is catalyzed into rotation back to the effulgence of summer. (Over time, the various festivals of light, such as Christmas and Hanukkah, were attracted to this archetypal motif like iron filings to a magnet). Any person, any culture that has a sense of participation in this great cycle feels a deep psycho-social-spiritual connection to a transpersonal energy. And any culture, such as ours, which has cut itself free from the cycle will suffer dread with aging and mortality, will feel rootless, adrift, and live as a stranger on this earth.

There in that dismal concavity, I felt linked through *the archetypal imagination* common to all humanity, linked to those distant predecessors, and reminded that we are all summoned to reconnect with those forces that lie outside our powers and in which we daily swim. We can thank those ancestors for their imaginal labor that now links our age with theirs, and Jung for describing the archetypal field of energy that allows us to stand in relationship to that which is larger than we. Immortal sap runs through the world tree, and while we are very mortal, perhaps we profit to remember our connection to the larger is best obtained through the archetypal imagination that courses within each of us.

Our branch of the evolutionary tree has survived because of its capacity to track these invisible energies, or at least to speculate upon them until better pictures emerge. While we have often fallen captive to our own constructions, thinking them the phenomena themselves, we are led by their autonomous transformations sooner or later to the more evolved pictures nature presents us. The German word for "imagination," *Einbildungskraft*, the "power of creating an image" illustrates; said affect-laden image then possesses the power to educate or inform consciousness. *Bildung*, sometimes loosely translated as "education," means the expectation that a person may acquire knowledge and capacity for choice, a range of cultural perspectives, and that he or she is adept in multiple disciplines, including the sciences and the arts. Originally, *Bild*, or "picture, image," intimated that this capacity for forming a picture manifested a human reflection of the mind and powers of Divinity.

As a more recent example, 19th-century poet and critic Samuel Taylor Coleridge differentiated *Primary Imagination*, *Secondary Imagination*, and *Fancy* to illustrate this agent of Divine *mimesis*. *Fancy* is what today we would call fashion, taste, aesthetics—what color the rug should be, given that couch and coffee table over there. *Secondary Imagination* is the echoing of the Divine act through the overt powers we exhibit in creating art, music, literature, architecture, theory, models, and so forth. The *Primary Imagination* lies in our elemental constitutive powers that Immanuel Kant, among others, identified as number, spatiality, sequence, and the like.

Additionally in the 19th century, both P. B. Shelley in his *A Defense of Poetry* and Arthur Schopenhauer in *The World as Will and Representation* speculated that it was the *imagination*, not reason, that made morality possible, opening us to em-pathy, sym-pathy, com-passion. While reason can differentiate, and divide, and categorize, imagination can intimate *the oneness beneath the disparity of things.*

Through our imaginative faculties, I am not wholly separate from you, and I can *imagine* your feelings, your pain, your suffering, and even experience them myself. Thus, the German *Mitleid*, the capacity to "suffer with" arises from the imaginal power, not the rational power.

So, too, quantum physics arises from alternative pictures as the context and our instrumentalities evolve, even those pictures that violate the received dictates of conventional reason: Neutrons *can* occupy multiple loci in an atom at the same time and without traversing the distance between orbits. Newtonian mechanics is a rich, pragmatic description but, for all its utility over the centuries, lacked sufficient imagination to encompass an ever-evolving mysterious universe. e. e. cummings titled a book of his poetry *is 5* because he wanted to remind us that there are universes where two plus two is 5. When Einstein was asked if he believed in "God," he replied, in a cable to Rabbi Herbert S. Goldstein, "*Spinoza's God*," suggesting that he was, like Newton, interested in reading the nature of things without necessarily positing a personality to it as well. And who, even more than cummings reminded us of the fictive nature of ego constructs, their relativity, than Einstein, Neils Bohr, Heisenberg, Pauli, and others who imagined a picture that might do justice to phenomena that simply refused to fit into the pictures that had worked rather well for centuries? (It is to the credit of science that it seems more willing to let go of its previous picture, far more willing than most theologians, when a better picture is required. When the Dali Lama was asked what he would do if science successfully challenged his beliefs, he said, "I would change my beliefs.").

In the end, we might repeat that archetypes form *psychic pictures of the world*—pictures that make familiar its smoky terrains, its terrifying declivities, its rolling chaos. In the end, the world *is as it is*, with or without us, but what we bring to it is a formative sensibility, an order, a purpose, and an evolving meaning. That in-forming order comes *from within us*, and *through us* into the world. It is not about us, but it is most uniquely us in the end. The archetypal imagination is what we modestly bring to help order history's disheveled table.

Each of our lives swirls through mystery from the first scattered shards of experience, through troubled islands of biography, across savannahs of suffering, to an unwelcomed dispersal back into the swirling universe. And yet, there is a kinship coursing beneath all beings, one in-forming energy. We carry it. It is implicate in all living things. Somehow, invisible tendrils reach out and connect all. Some have called this energy "love," at least what Dante called "*the Love that moves the sun and the other stars.*"

It is as if we are all serving a calling, an unfolding of energy that was meant to be embodied, even as we are, all the while, the humble instruments to bring it into the world. Rather than ask, *why am I here*—and society has provided us many self-estranging answers to that question—might we better ask the question: "*What wants to enter the world through me?*" Is it not better to reflect on what our incarnation might mean, not from our ego or cultural positions, but from the standpoint of nature, or of divinity? Is not our calling, then, to serve that purpose, even as it may prove costly to fitting in, ego comfort, or anxiety-driven agendas? As my good friend, poet Stephen Dunn explained in his poem "The Prayer You Asked For":

> *I want you to trust*
> *that belief doesn't matter to me now,*
>
> *only love does in this grand unruly scheme*
> *of our lives together.*[6]

Elinor Lerman's poem "*There Is a Woman Standing on a Terrace*" reminds us that, however obscure, however recondite, however incognito our passages, it is all as it is meant to be. And an awareness of the archetypal forms rolling beneath us makes it possible that even the most foreign is now seen as both friend and invitation:

> *There is a woman standing on a terrace. She is*
> *wearing a silk sheath—green I think; as pale as*
> *tea. She is holding a drink so icy that it tastes*
> *like mercury. The Pleiades are overhead and she*
> *is gazing eastward, toward the South China Sea.*

---

[6] Shared with me in an email. At this writing, unpublished.

How do you know? Because this is after,
After all your work is done, after the passing of
so many, the travel that took you nowhere.
After you married and divorced, after your children
defied you, which meant that you had done your job.

Now you are so old that you are free to hope.
Nothing needs to be considered except the root
of your desire, which has become that
crystal sliver of pain that all the doctors told you
was a chronic headache but you suspect might be
the original nerve still pulsing, the ache
that has been with you, always.

So eat breakfast. Pack lightly. Then start your journey
to the deep water city, to the hotel on a hill above Repulse
Bay.
What does it matter that you were "never meant to be
here?"
What does it matter that when you speak to her she
will answer in French? You will be able to understand her

if you want to, and she will know who you are.
Bring her a drink that tastes of melon. And as the sky
hangs out its starry animals—a fish, a bear,
a canny dog—tell her how long it took to form
these constellations. That human beings have named them.
That anything is possible and that you, you are the proof.[7]

[7] "There is a Woman Standing on a Terrace," Eleanor Lerman from *Our Post-Soviet History Unfolds*. Sarabande https://writersalmanac.publicradio.org/index.php%3Fdate=2006%252F06%252F10.html

Chapter Two
Reframing Our Sense of Self and World in Plague Times

"Go to, they are not men o' their words: they told me
I was everything; 'tis a lie — I am not ague-proof."
Shakespeare, *King Lear*, 4/5.

Pressed as he so often was to define his concept of the Divine, Jung relented and said he called "God" that which flung itself violently across our path and alters our conscious intentions for good or for ill. This is a very peculiar definition of Divinity; however, the more I have struggled with it, the more profound, the more inescapable, it seems.

The human ego, tasked with interacting with the outer world, so often imagines itself Big Boss, the Emperor of Impulse, the Diviner of Desire, and the Czar of Choice. All the while it is a fragile cluster of energy, full of tergiversations, contradictions, swirling fears, rationalizations, excuses, and shabby justifications.

And for every act of its putative sovereignty, the ego is mocked by the vast powers in which it floats. Frequently invaded, it has little sense of consistency, and yet, and yet, it imagines itself in charge like the flea that is simply bigger than other fleas. In his peculiar definition of Divinity, Jung pivots to recognize the majestic otherness of the Other, to reposition the imperialistic ego, and to teach it a lesson or two—the kind of lesson that came to hyper-pious, presumptive Job before his life and his Weltanschauung collapsed. This recognition of the infinitude and autonomy of the absolute Other is true piety and true respect for human limits.

Putting it simply, Jung is saying that whenever our ego frame collapses, we are in the presence of the mystery of the large, radical *Other*. Whenever we are obliged to radically reframe our sense of self and world, we are in the presence of mystery. Anything short of that is evidence that the ego is up to its old tricks, seeking to hedge its bets, compromise, slither away. Whatever calls the ego consciousness to encounter its limitations and open to the reframing of understanding is, according to Jung, a religious encounter. So, beware of asking for religious experience. You might get one.

Given this incredibly inflated understanding of where we stand in the cosmos, we may say that our traumatic encounter with the Covid-19 pandemic is a Divine encounter—not as a punishment from an anthropomorphic character sitting upstairs judging all below, not as a refutation to further presumptive beliefs, but as a GPS summons to recalculate the actual position of the ego, and human life in general, in the larger scheme of mystery. As individuals have had to sequester, lose contact with their normal pursuits, and encounter their powerlessness against something a thousand times smaller than a grain of salt, they have had to go back to their metaphysical drawing board in so many ways. It will be interesting to see what long-term changes and such recalculations bring to individual lives and our social structures.

It is a central dynamic of the human psyche that the less we know of an object, a person, a situation, a context, the more we flood it with our projections. Projections are our way of trying to finesse the vacuum of ignorance, make sense of it, and bring to bear whatever strategies our history has taught us. *Projection* means I am always dealing with aspects of myself "out there," on the Other, though I believe I am operating in an objective way with that Other. *Transference* means I bring my past strategies to bear on the new situation in service to making sense of it and perhaps bring it under the wing of our sovereignty. But when the Other refuses to cooperate, when its "otherness" wears away the expectations of the projections, then a higher dollop of anxiety rises from a destabilized ego. In the Western world, we are so used to having our marvelous scientists swoop in and explain why that plane went down or offer us a pill to take care of the problem—all these reassuring palliative steps to return us to the expectation of "normality" as soon as possible.

It is easy to see this in the case histories of the past and how quickly we feel superior to our superstitious predecessors. When the Black Death came to Europe in 1348-49 and left up to 40 percent of the population dead, and all its institutions rendered impotent, there were efforts to find magic, find culprits, engage in exorcisms of one sort or another. Some joined the parades of the flagellants who wandered the countryside lashing themselves to cleanse themselves of the sin they believed had caused the horror. In August 1349, to choose one example, the good citizens of Mainz, Germany, turned on their neighbors the Jews and murdered 6,000 of them. (I am sure that purgation did wonders to end *Die Pest* quickly).

In our "progressive" time, our dysfunctional and self-interested leaders have ignored the problem, discarded scientific evidence and methodology, blamed other countries, alleged hoaxes and conspiracies, turned to wackadoodle cures like bleach and off-the-label meds, lied, blamed, were deliberately duplicitous, and generally acted much like the ignorant leaders of the world in the 14th century. Back then, no one thought to blame germs, for who could believe in something one could not see, even imagine. No one thought to look to the fleas on the backs of the omnipresent rats. We didn't even have those excuses. We know about germs, bacteria, and viruses, we have centuries of data in dealing with pandemics, yet the technique which ultimately freed Europe—social distancing—was the best we have until vaccines made their appearance on the scene, long after hundreds of thousands had died. But we were too stupid, too selfish, too self-indulgent to profit from all this knowledge. So much for progress! So, we are now obliged to learn that when reality obliges the reframing of our paradigms, it is time to let go of the old and seek a better frame.

As hideous as this pandemic has been with its mounting toll of the dead and wounded, what metastasizes most in these situations is human fear, blaming, denial, self-medication, scapegoating, and distraction—just like in the good old days of the Black Death.

After all, we are so big now, aren't we? And why would we take little viruses seriously? Why we can't even see the little buggers. And what we can't see we certainly aren't going to take seriously. Even so, the irrepressible fears released like balloons that slip from the hands of a child, rise, embroider, and engulf us in their threat. I have no cure for this dilemma. It is human nature thrown back upon itself, stripped of its phanticized sovereignty. But it is, remembering Jung, in such moments that one is invited to radically reframe one's sense of self and other.

To recover our standpoint, we need to acknowledge the role that fear and anxiety play in our lives. I know it sounds reductionistic, but fear management techniques of all kinds constitute most of our agendas most of the time. Fear itself is not the problem. Fear is part of our evolutionary equipment for survival. It is, after all, a lethal world in which we find ourselves. Just now ... did that movement of the bush over there come from our kinsman returning home from the hunt bringing us our dinner, or is it the tiger that is planning on us for dinner?

Those who have studied such matters say that apparently the only fear we all have inherently is the fear of falling. All infants reveal a panic reaction when they are dropped. All other fears are learned somehow along the way. We carry all that history with us, organized in clusters called "complexes," shards of experience that are activated by any new visitant seen from the perspective of the old frame. Some of our complexes are helpful, supportive; some are pernicious and infantilizing. But all complexes, to some degree, 1) pull us out of this moment, 2) relocate us in the time and context of its creation, and 3) link us to the understanding, the limited frame, and the constrained behavior of that time, that place, and frequently, the powerlessness of that distant hour. All complexes are "stories," not the reality, but the constructs, the narratives, the fragmentary interpretations of the mysterious world around us, and not the reality itself. Unwittingly, we become captives of our constructs, not the world as it is, but how we structure it, construe it, try to make sense of it.

In the discipline of General Semantics, there is a truism: "The map is not the territory." If I pulled out a map of, say, Oklahoma, and took the map for the territory, then I could step over Oklahoma in a single bound. Reportedly, Picasso was once upbraided at a party for not painting his human figures as they "really" looked. He ask his critic to show him a picture of his family. He looked closely at the photo and said, "My, you have a tiny family." In other words, the critic was able to accept one construct, the photo, with no problem, but could not accept the artist's construct. Accordingly, our complexes overlay the reality, are as much construings of reality as our eyeglass lenses are, but we accept the world they present as the real world, the objective reality.

While all our stories are "logical" within their bounds, they are seldom rational or objective. Thus, we never do "crazy" things when in the grip of a complex; we do "logical" things, given the premise of the lens through which we see things. Human reason, which remembers these limits, is fragile in the face of the rush of the hour and is usually forgotten when fear is evoked. Nature gave us the tools of fight, flight, or freeze to cope with an immense Other. When we see that Other through the reductive lens of our history, the more magnified its otherness. The more distanced from our conscious life, the more irrational, more regressive in its message it is likely to be. The earlier the triggered complex in our formative history, the more primitive its attending script and the more limited our resources to contain it. Thus, the stresses of the plague or other boundary-breaking experiences will likely launch regressive responses from us *or* may in fact summon us to an enlargement of our philosophy of self and world. As we all know, comfort, control, and predictability lull the spirit, even as adversity stretches it and demands growth. [add i to spirit] We live in such a time. (As the medieval aphorism reminds us, "suffering is the fastest horse to completion.")

Let us remember for a moment the difference between *fear* and *anxiety*. Fear is specific: the fear of fire, the fear of heights, and so on. Anxiety is amorphous, vague, abstract even. It is like the fog that crosses the highway. Put your hand into that fog, and there is no "there" there, but it can block your way. Thus, it can be a moment of profound liberation to look into the fog of anxiety and identify specific fears there.

The triggering of fear or anxiety also triggers our history, specifically our complexes, and frequently catastrophizes. Recently I was discussing his stress with an American businessman of Middle Eastern heritage and how he so frequently gets engulfed by life's normal problems. While he is a man of considerable talent, intellect, and gifts of coping, he is easily flooded, loses sleep, and feels debilitated. Sadly, his encounter with stupid and bigoted playmates, reinforced occasionally by other, more adult idiots, created in him a fractured sense of security, sense of personal legitimacy, and sense of permission to be who he really is. So, someone else's ignorance, stupidity, and fear become a defining frame for his contemporary stresses. The activation of that history obliges him to ignore his conscientious management of his business and his life and feel at the mercy of others, even though he is quite prudent and secure in reality. To be able to identify, track, and address those childhood traumas and watch how they feed the catastrophizing fears of the present is profoundly freeing. The old fears don't go away, but he remains less and less an automatic victim of them. So, too, each of us has been triggered in plague times and all our archaic fears aroused like wolves howling out on the dark prairie.

When we recognize the presence of the archaic fear, we also have to recognize 1) it is not likely to happen in reality, and 2) were it to happen, we have the emotional, legal, and fiscal resources to cope with the threat quite well. The odds of actual problems proving catastrophic are minimal, but the old world frame does not know that, and so the capacities of the adult who is now present to protect the frightened child within is flooded and knocked off center.

In Martell's popular novel and film, *The Life of Pi*, a study of fear, the author tells us:

> I must say a word about fear. It is life's only true opponent. Only fear can defeat life. It is a clever, treacherous adversary, how well I know. It has no decency, respects no law or convention, shows no mercy. It goes for your weakest spot, which it finds with unerring ease … if your fear becomes a wordless darkness that you avoid, perhaps even manage to forget, you open yourself to further attacks of fear because you never truly fought the opponent who defeated you.

What I and other therapists have found through the decades is that fear, usually archaic fear—which is to say, formed early in our evolving sense of self and world—dictates so many of our behaviors. It is the secret god we worship with devotion, fidelity, and vigilance, because that "god" once came to the child and demanded obedience forever.

Let us look at two well-known poems that address fear and the role it plays in the governance of our lives. The first poem is titled "Snake" and is written by D. H. Lawrence after an experience he had in 1922 in Sicily, beneath the hovering presence of smoldering Mount Aetna. Read the poem aloud to yourself, slowly, allow the images to rise in your mind's eye, and then we will talk about it.

Snake

A snake came to my water-trough
On a hot, hot day, and I in pajama's for the heat,
To drink there.
In the deep, strange-scented shade of the great dark carob tree
I came down the steps with my pitcher
And must wait, must stand and wait, for there he was at the trough before me.
He reached down from a fissure in the earth-wall in the gloom
And trailed his yellow-brown slackness soft-bellied down, over the edge of the stone trough
And rested his throat upon the stone bottom,
And where the water had dripped from the tap, in a small clearness,

He sipped with his straight mouth,
Softly drank through his straight gums, into his slack
long body,
Silently.
Someone was before me at my water-trough,
And I, like a second-comer, waiting.
He lifted his head from his drinking, as cattle do,
And looked at me vaguely, as drinking cattle do,
And flickered his two-forked tongue from his lips, and
mused a moment,
And stooped and drank a little more,
Being earth-brown, earth-golden from the burning
bowels of the earth
On the day of Sicilian July, with Etna smoking.
The voice of my education said to me
He must be killed,
For in Sicily the black, black snakes are innocent, the
gold are venomous.
And voices in me said, If you were a man
You would take a stick and break him now, and finish
him off.
But must I confess how I liked him,
How glad I was he had come like a guest in quiet, to
drink at my water-trough
And depart peaceful, pacified, and thankless,
Into the burning bowels of this earth?
Was it cowardice, that I dared not kill him?
Was it perversity, that I longed to talk to him?
Was it humility, to feel honoured?
I felt so honoured.

And yet those voices:
If you were not afraid you would kill him.
And truly I was afraid, I was most afraid,
But even so, honoured still more
That he should seek my hospitality
From out the dark door of the secret earth.
He drank enough
And lifted his head, dreamily, as one who has drunken,
And flickered his tongue like a forked night on the air, so black,
Seeming to lick his lips,
And looked around like a god, unseeing, into the air,
And slowly turned his head,
And slowly, very slowly, as if thrice adream,
Proceeded to draw his slow length curving round
And climb again the broken bank of my wall-face.
And as he put his head into that dreadful hole,
And as he slowly drew up, snake-easing his shoulders, and entered further,
A sort of horror, a sort of protest against his
withdrawing into that horrid black hole,
Deliberately going into the blackness, and slowly
drawing himself after,
Overcame me now his back was turned.
I looked round, I put down my pitcher,
I picked up a clumsy log
And threw it at the water-trough with a clatter.
I think it did not hit him,
But suddenly that part of him that was left behind
convulsed in undignified haste,

Writhed like lightning, and was gone
Into the black hole, the earth-lipped fissure in the wall-
front,
At which, in the intense still noon, I stared with
fascination.
And immediately I regretted it.
I thought how paltry, how vulgar, what a mean act!
I despised myself and the voices of my accursèd human
education.
And I thought of the albatross,
And I wished he would come back, my snake.
For he seemed to me again like a king,
Like a king in exile, uncrowned in the underworld,
Now due to be crowned again.
And so, I missed my chance with one of the lords
Of life.
And I have something to expiate:
A pettiness.

First, think of your own associations with the word *snake*. Some people love snakes, some are indifferent, and most people are frightened by snakes. They are visitants from the underworld, even as our dreams are. As such, snakes are often seen as affronts to the ego's presumed mastery of the outer world. Even though that ego fantasy is continuously overthrown both by demands of that outer world and the insurgencies of complexes, dreams, repetitive patterns from below, the ego perpetually wishes to be the boss. So here in "Snake," we are told, is this disruptive visitant to "our" world. Really? Or is it the reverse. Who got here first?

Lawrence goes on marvelously to describe the conflict within him. He feels honored by the encounter with one of the Lords of Life, and yet "the voices of his education," the oughts and shoulds with which we all grew up, counsels aggression. (Fight, flight, or freeze). Even more, the voice of his cultural formation, activating the amygdala, the most primitive part of the brain, commands him as a "man" to be aggressive and dispatch the intruder. The tension of opposites in the speaker is an impressive and compelling saga, a story all of us have experienced sometime in our life. The amygdala and the frontal cortex, the more evolved, more "conscious," more civilized part of his brain, are at war with each other.

And then something snaps in him. He throws the log, the snake slips into the depths, and the tension is broken. Then, perhaps surprising to the reader who identified with the threat, the speaker condemns himself for his fear-driven response, and realizes that he, graced by an encounter with the mystery of the other world, blew it, and succumbed to his most primitive fears. How often this regressive reaction is felt in all of us, and from time to time, we have the power to look back at it, and realize we were afraid of risk, afraid of commitment, afraid of revealing what we really felt, afraid of being who we wanted to be. And the moment is passed. Sometimes forever.

Recognizing this regressive response in himself, the speaker condemns himself to a high crime and misdemeanor: pettiness. He equates himself with Coleridge's ancient mariner, who must carry the burden of his impulsive choice around his neck in perpetuity and serve the contrition it asks of him. Our soul often has high desires, and we have petty offerings in return. The costs slowly mount, and the unlived life slips slowly into the shadowy areas of the room.

To me, the most important word in the entire poem, apart from *snake*, is the word *deliberately*. You may have missed it. Please go back and look at the word: "deliberately going into the blackness." I think the fulcrum of the poem is that word *deliberately*. There, in that instant, the ego is summoned to the *catabasis*, the descent into the underworld, such as we all carry within us. And, as we so often do, he flees the invitation. The snake's toxicity is not its venom; it is its reminder of the vibrant world below our world. In a letter Jung once observed that the dread and resistance we all have to entering the unconscious is understandable because it can be the voyage to Hades. That said, we carry those depths within us, we rose from them, and are always experiencing invasions from them. To run from their encounter is to run from ourselves, to run from depth, and to abide in the superficial distractions of outer life.

I have above my desk a postcard sent me many years ago, back in the early '80s. I had finished my training as an analyst in Zürich and was back in America. My Swiss analyst, Dr. Adolf Ammann, and his wife Yolanda made their only visit to this hemisphere. They wanted to see two things: Disney World and the Grand Canyon. I was moved to receive from him a postcard of the Grand Canyon at night. A full moon hangs above the rim of the canyon, and the layers of that archetypal terrain progressively move downward from those visible by lunar light at the top to those shrouded in the dark below. It is an impressive photograph. He wrote one sentence, with his initials A. A., on the back side: "Who would ever go down there!"

I was touched by his remembering me while in the presence of the attractions of the new world, but even more, moved by his loving reminder to me, as I interpreted his remark: "*we go down there*. That is our work. That is what depth psychology does—engages those deeper layers." It was a call, a reminder of this work, this profession, this summons we all have in our lives.

So, when we come back to that word *deliberately*, I think we see why the speaker snapped. No right-thinking person would go down there—that is the place of the depths. Our own mind, as poet G. M. Hopkins said, confronts us with "cliffs of sheer fall / no man-fathomed." But, to his credit, the speaker of the poem, and Lawrence himself, is mature enough to recognize and be accountable for the flight from the depths such as we experience in many ways. Such an admission is all we can ask of an adult.

So, for us, too, the invitation occasioned by sequestering, the loss of the familiar in plague times requires that we engage our own depths, to deal with and be accountable for whatever comes up from below—fears, insights, primitive flights, new energies. That is all we can ask of an adult. So, for each of us during these difficult times, or other difficult times to come, there will be many metaphoric serpents appearing at our door, asking us to go deeper into life than we had planned. And how we respond will make a large, large difference in the journey we call our life.

Another poem altogether is Marsha Truman Cooper's "Fearing Paris."

Fearing Paris
Suppose that what you fear
could be trapped
and held in Paris.
Then you would have
the courage to go
everywhere in the world.
All the directions of the compass
open to you,
except the degrees east or west
of true north
that lead to Paris.
Still, you wouldn't dare
put your toes
smack dab on the city limit line.
You're not really willing
to stand on a mountainside,
miles away,
and watch the Paris lights
come up at night.
Just to be on the safe side,
you decide to stay completely
out of France.
But then danger
seems too close
even to those boundaries,
and you feel
the timid part of you
covering the whole globe again.
You need the kind of friend
who learns your secret and says,
"See Paris first."

Here, the flight which protected the speaker in Lawrence's poem is countered by the opposite advice: *Go into the fear, deal with it, lest you live a fugitive life.* So many of us are fugitives, furtive denizens of exile and estrangement. As analyst, I can only help recognize the role that fear is playing in the client's stuckness, the price of avoidance, the accumulating cost of a constricted life. What so often happens is that over time the ego consciousness gathers more evidence, discerns the cost of flight, and recognizes the need for change.

So often, folks come in, wholly defended against acknowledging the deadness of their marriages or the cumulative cost of habitual behaviors, the rising toll of avoidance, but finally decide to act. German philosopher Heidegger once observed that "the horrible has already happened." I take his remark to mean that the child's encounter with the traumatic magnitude of life's demands has already wreaked its woe, and after that we have only the path upward to something better.

The thing I fear is my greatest challenge, and the fear I push through is an aperture into the larger life my soul demands. When we mobilize courage, resolve, and finally act, then one can sit again on the banks of the Seine, watch the lover's locks on the bridges, hear the accordion music waft over the evening, sip a glass of merlot, and finally, finally really be here in life.

****

Having paid attention to these matters for a few decades, it seems clear to me that the human psyche seems to want two things:

- The fullest possible expression of its potential
- Self-healing

When fear manages our lives, and it does a good deal of the time, we are then cast over against ourselves and are divided souls. Healing only happens when we push through those fears into the more capacious life that awaits. Jung noted that our personal religions are found where we *really* worship, that is, where we invest the most energy. It's fair to say, then, that our *deepest* religious service goes to our fear-management systems.

Having learned early the magnitude of the world and its powers, we quickly adapt to fit in and evolve a functional personality. This adaptive personality, or false self, has two goals:

- Get our needs met as best we can
- Manage our fears as best we can

Jung wrote of a patient who came to him having visited many physicians before him. He was convinced that he was dying of a terminal cancer. Jung examined him and agreed with his dire self-diagnosis: His cancer was his metastasizing anxiety. He believed his cancer-fear was eating his body when in fact it was eating his soul. What were his real fears within? We don't know, but we are probably on safe ground to assume they were the fear of life itself! Similarly, in his essay on the "Soul and Death," Jung noted that those who most feared death were those who were most consumed by a fear of life itself, and those most able to accept the end of their journey were those who had most lived it. Our common condition is mortality, as we all know, and the fear of the tiny, invisible virus, or its many variations in the carousel of life, are enough to shut us down early, and life is already lost then. Life is a loan, and we have to return it to the universe. Ironically, only when we accept our mortality can we work backward to this present moment and perhaps live more fully while we are here—now!

Paradoxically, we gain some sovereignty back when we acknowledge our powerlessness over mortality and thereby are gifted with more resolve to live fully *here*, in the immediacy of *now*. The 17th-century philosopher/inventor/mystic Blaise Pascal once wrote:

> "*Man is a reed, the weakest of nature, but he is a thinking reed. It is not necessary that the entire universe arm itself to crush: a vapor, a drop of water suffices to kill him. But if the universe were to crush him, man would still be nobler than what kills him, because he knows that he dies and the advantage that the universe has over him, the universe knows nothing of this.*"

It seems ironic, prescient that he uses the phrase *vapor*, or *drop of water*, for in this hour when we are now alerted to the aerosols that carry the virus, the tiny, invisible droplets of the final democracy of all mortals. But the key then is this: What does that recognition make us *do*, or *keep* us from doing with our lives? Do our fears sharpen our consciousness, trigger our resolve toward personal sovereignty, or do they make us fugitives in our own lives?

Our fears ultimately lead us back to ourselves, and we often fear that isolation, that aloneness. And yet the flight from our aloneness leads us further and further from ourselves.

Our social distancing is an enormous invitation to make better friends with ourselves, to dialogue with our inner lives. The pandemic has obliged all of us to now be introduced unwillingly to an inner life, and many do not like the person they meet there.

* * * *

Our personal and societal experience of the pandemic raises many collective questions, questions which affect all of us. Will there be long-term changes to our society? Or will the lessons of this troubled hour be forgotten quickly in the rush to "normalize" and move back into a world of distractions? Of course, it is the nature of our nature to prefer order to disorder, predictability, and demand a measure of control. This pandemic flies in the face of all that. An organism one thousand times smaller than a grain of sand is more powerful than the masters of the earth? Go figure. ...

Yet, the rush to get back to "normal" has revealed an immaturity, a flaw in our character. Our narcissistic self-interests demand the resumption of our previous lifestyle even in the face of reason, knowledge, and the lethality of making the wrong choice. Not since World War II has there been such a threat to each North American, a phenomenon that touches all of us, invades our homes, our jobs, our minds. Yes, there have been many other national events: walking on the moon, the murder of a president, the Challenger explosion, 9/11, but they were all "out there," "over there," touching others perhaps, but few of us directly and immediately.

We all have made adjustments, but it is also clear that catalyzed complexes rise to the surface in the face of such threats. Who would have imagined that medical facts would be denied in a nation that prides itself on its sciences? Who would have imagined the moral bankruptcy of our national leadership, which chose political expediency over lives? Who would have imagined that wearing a simple face mask would be a political rather than medical issue? It reminds one of H. L. Mencken's remark that you can't go broke underestimating the intelligence of the American people. Heretofore, I might have contended with his remark, but not today.

The toll of lives lost, families destroyed, jobs disappeared is staggering, and their consequences will go on for many years. The oppression of the disease and its *sequelae* certainly beget depression, and often impulsive actions ranging from violence to increased self-medication, to relational animosities. All of these are expected, and lamentable, and all are keeping therapists, bartenders, and delivery services busy—for those who can afford them, but what are some of the possible changes that we *may* be noting in our cultural perspectives:

1. No doubt, there will be greater respect for telecommunications, teletherapy, in-home schooling, and the like. For just one example, hitherto professional societies and insurance corporations frowned on teletherapy. But, as we know, necessity is the mother of invention, and that shibboleth is probably broken

forever. As a result, less car pollution, less time wasted looking for parking places, less office rent, and more opportunity for those in distant places to avail themselves of resources once denied them by geography, not to mention, an enormous savings on office clothes. (Friend and therapist Kat Wilderotter said the new normal for office attire, after the virus passes, will be exercise bottoms, T-shirt tops, sneakers, but if one is occupying an executive role, the socks should match).

2. I would like to believe—even if certain politicians may still be around—that we might evolve as a society with a greater respect for *expertise* in all fields. The denigration of "science" and professionalism has proved very costly in blood and treasure. In the face of widespread ignorance, superstition, gullibility in the face of internet trolls, there is such a thing as knowledge, and knowledge may in fact free us.

3. The incredible disparity of access to saving resources has again revealed the egregious separation of haves and have-nots in terms of access to health care, computers, internet, and so on, even in a country that prides itself on its democratic vision. This horrible discrepancy between our professed values *may* lead to some greater sharing of our wealth. But I won't bet against the self-interest of the haves prevailing, as they have so many times before.

4. We seem now to have greater appreciation of so many who are so imperiled on the front lines of our society … not only the physicians and nurses, but those

delivering goods, working in grocery stores—all essential workers. Possibly some reduction in our stratified educational and economic snobbery will erode a bit. Again, I may be expecting too much. All I know is those good folks have been keeping us alive, feeding us, bringing us more junk to fill our homes, and in general dying far more often than the likely readers of this essay.

5. We all recall self-proclaimed American philosopher Ronald Reagan facilely saying that the scariest sentence was: "Hi, I'm from the government and I'm here to help." But attitudes change when the hurricane has leveled your city, when the virus is rampant, and when incompetence and ignorance prevail at local levels. Now we know that only a government of the people and on behalf of the people large enough and expert enough to tackle really large problems is necessary. The hodgepodge and contradictions of local authorities has led to many more dead. Assuredly, there is blood on the hands of those who at the state and federal levels chose politics over the health of their constituents, or fealty to political subservience.

6. I recently saw a political cartoon where a person said, "I wish COVID would leave so I could get back to incessantly worrying about global warming." When we come to ongoing problems such as racism, economic disparities, global warming, we instantly hear that we do not have the resources, either of people or cash to address these issues. Would that economic distribution of resources and national will might be mobilized to

address these problems, which will survive long after the virus is gone.

7. Hopefully, some people, forced out of routine, deprived of their usual distractions, found some new interests, rediscovered old ones left behind, such as reading and conversing, and that some folks made better friends with themselves simply because they had to. Human resourcefulness, a sense of humor, imagination, and sheer pragmatism are impressive when they surface.

I do expect, however, for a least a generation or two, that those going through this great time of uncertainty and threat, will take fewer things for granted, won't casually assume that systems will always work, that food, health, and entertainment streams will flow uninterruptedly, and we will have a more realistic view of the contingencies and fragility of human life. We can readily identify problems that require our mature responses; it is something else to shift resources and commitment in those directions once the heat is off. Above all, we cannot afford complacency and naiveté because in difficult times, they will kill us.

* * * *

Pascal observed that most folks considered the gravest threat to their mental comfort was being with themselves in their private chambers for an extended period. How many of our contemporary tribe flip out if the internet goes down or Netflix is off or their cell phones are on the fritz. Recently, one of my clients told me her grandson was incredulous that she had grown up not only without TV but without cell phones. "But how did you talk to each other, Grandma," he asked? Our present plague-time situation is no different than at all other times; it's simply that we have more distractions to help us ignore the fragility of the human condition. With enough distractions humans can divert their gaze from anything, from anything. And what a nightmare when one can't distract.

When reading Viktor Frankl's *Man's Search for Meaning*, his first-person account of his time in a concentration camp, the horror of losing his family, his freedom, his dignity, I was stunned when he said that as terrible as Auschwitz was, it was but an hyperbolic expression of everyday life. I believe what he meant was that in daily life, as in Auschwitz, everything, everything we count on, everything that supports us, can be taken from us in an instant. And, yet, he argued, in both that terrible place and our more familiar places of occasional terror, we are accountable for our attitudes and practices, and that meaning arises out of our values and our choices to live them. From his searing experience, he developed *Logotherapy*, a treatment based on the perception that we are creatures who cannot live without meaning. While we may have our family, our possessions, all taken from us, we may retain our inner freedom, our enduring integrity in the face of all. While this idea fills me with dread, I know it is true and believe it points the path forward.

In my last book about finding personal resilience in changing times, I expressed this summons:

Jung put it best when he wrote, "The highest and most decisive experience of all … is to be alone with … [one's] own self, or whatever else one chooses to call the objectivity of the psyche. The patient must be alone if he is to find out what it is that supports him when he can no longer support himself. Only this experience can give him an indestructible foundation." Another way to phrase that may be that we need to find what supports us when nothing supports us. That is, when the experience of the loss of the other is upon us and we are flush with separation anxiety, rather than run to the nearest safe harbor, we sit with it and sit it out. During that time, we learn, to our surprise, that something rises within to support us. We will not perish though we think we will. By bearing the unbearable, we go "through" the desert to arrive at a nurturing oasis we did not know was there.[8]

In this ongoing opus of self-governance, we need to begin by recontextualizing our fears and reframing them, lest their presuppositions prove tragically wrong. So, we must remember these things on a daily basis:

We are *always* mortal, *always* in peril. That is the status of daily life, but the real question is: Do we retain a personal *dignity*, a personal *integrity*, or do we live furtive and fugitive lives? Our parents, our children, ourselves—all of us—are on the same journey. Why should I think myself exempt?

---

[8] James Hollis, *Living Between Worlds: Finding Personal Resilience in Changing Times.*, p. 124.

These life conundrums always remain with us, even as our tool kit may grow larger and larger:

Can you ask of yourself:

- Am I *living* my life or not showing up at all?
- Is my journey diminished by fear and by my collusion with that fear?
- Is fear the *driver*, and do I learn from time to time to stand up and risk being who I am regardless of the cost, regardless of the voices calling me back to a fugitive life?
- Where do I need to stand up now? Show up now?
- Did I remember to love and serve those around me?
  (In Albert Camus' *The Plague*, the protagonist, Dr. Rieux says that sometimes the most decent thing to do is simply do your job, be counted on, show up where you are needed).
- Have I learned that I, too, am *equipped* for this journey, provided the same tools, same resilience, and same tenacity that pulled my ancestors through?

Those who ask these questions and risk new practices—one of which being simply to sit and be present to one's soul without interventions from others—will actually grow larger from this terrible time of threat and depredation. Those who flee this summons will be stuck with the old frame, the old evasions, the old self-soothing, and never experience the gift of a deeper, more interesting journey. They will never know that this larger life, lived fully in the presence of uncertainty, mortality, and rising congeries of challenge was offered them, but they didn't show up and step onto the field.

If we return a moment to Jung's definition of "God," then we realize that we have all been brought by this virus into the presence of that which has violently invaded our presumptive worlds, altered our conscious plans for better or worse, and brought us all to new places we hadn't planned to visit. In those engagements, we are in the presence of something large, really large, and we have to meet it with something more than our old, safe, small, and familiar plans.

Chapter Three
Who Heals the Healer? —
The Profile of the Wounded Healer

"The very angels themselves cannot persuade the
wretched and blundering children on the earth as can
one human being broken on the wheels of living.
In love's service, only the wounded soldiers can serve."
  Thornton Wilder, *The Angel That Troubled the Waters.*

There is a wounded part in all of us, and there is a healing
part in all of us. From those centers, whether we know it or
not, choices rise, patterns begin, and the unconscious engines
of choice create our histories. While this essay was first
delivered as a speech/workshop for professional caregivers,
many who did not fit that occupational designation found that
it spoke to them as well. Are not most of us in relationships
where wounded parts of us are repeatedly activated, and are
most of us not also in relationships where we seek the healing
of others? So, this essay is for more than therapists, nurses,
clergy, social workers, and the like. It is for all of us: a
reminder, a caution, and perhaps a help.

The Archetype of the Wounded Healer

While found in all cultures in various stories, the work, risk, gift, and cost of healing finds its mythic origin in the confession of Asclepius, the Greek physician who, in recognition of his own wounds, established a retreat for healers at Epidaurus where they might repair and be healed of their own wounds. Little is known of that sanctuary, but what little we do know tells us the following. As *sanctuary*, one has already effected a break from the people, places, and things that were part of the mounting stresses that afflict the healer.

Those seeking healing found "*incubation*" through sacred space and restoration of psyche's balance.

Apparently, they indulged in *cleansing baths*, a symbolic regression to the restorative powers of the unconscious and the archetypal fount of our origins. They were told to pay attention to their dreams as compensatory messages from the unconscious. Even bites from nonlethal serpents in the area were welcomed for quickening consciousness and, presumably, for healing encounters with the balm of the Great Mother, as we witnessed in the D. H. Lawrence poem earlier.

Jung thought a great deal about the psychology of the wounded healer. In this diagram, simple as it appears, are 12 different vectors of energy.

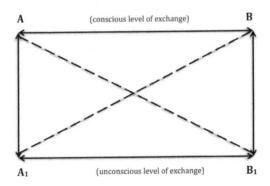

At the top level we see two people relating to each other consciously, as this writer and you the reader are. But both of us brought all of who we are into this moment also. Some of that massive data dump is activated in any given moment, which is to say the two sidelines are lit up, triggering the unconscious, which floods the conscious person with some variant of the question: "Where have I been here before?" The data from the past floods the consciousness of person A or B and influences their choices. It also inevitably falls back into the unconscious.

Additionally, the diagonal lines indicate how the unconscious material is projected onto the other person or situation. The contents of the unconscious can either continue to flood the other, distorting their reality, or return to the unconscious. Once again, the energy vector flows both ways.

And, at the deepest level, the unconscious of one person is affecting the unconscious of the other. We all know that some relationships are inherently healing or iatrogenic, depending on what material, what historical script, has been catalyzed. This simple diagram, flowing in 12 directions simultaneously, helps explain the healing or wounding effects of our relationships, the creation of their patterns, and why so many end up in the dead end of repetition.

In examining the profile of and strategies of the wounded healer, Jung concluded that half of any depth treatment consists of the healer examining herself or himself and that healing can only take place if the healer has a relationship with his/her own unconscious. For "only what he can put right in himself can be put right in the patient."[9]

Of course, the healing task is *dangerous* because it opens the healer up to the toxins coursing within the other, whether of physical or psychological nature. Yet, "it is his own hurt that gives the measure of his/her power to heal … this is the meaning of the Greek myth of the wounded healer."[10]

As we all know, prolonged exposure to pathologies of all kinds, including racism, sexism, bigotry, poverty, and many others begin to fill one's soul like invisible silica drifting down from the ceiling. Even the routinization of office life can provide such incremental intoxification, as Theodore Roethke reveals in his precomputer poem "Dolor."

I have known the inexorable sadness of pencils,
Neat in their boxes, dolor of pad and paper weight,
All the misery of manila folders and mucilage,
Desolation in immaculate public places,
Lonely reception room, lavatory, switchboard,
The unalterable pathos of basin and pitcher,
Ritual of multigraph, paper-clip, comma,
Endless duplication of lives and objects.
And I have seen dust from the walls of institutions,
Finer than flour, alive, more dangerous than silica,
Sift, almost invisible, through long afternoons of tedium,

<hr>

[9] Jung, CW 16, *The Development of the Personality.* "Fundamental Questions of Psychotherapy," para. 239.
[10] *Ibid.*

Dropping a fine film on nails and delicate eyebrows,
Glazing the pale hair, the duplicate grey standard faces.

In the ancient healing arts of shamanism, the healer was
sometimes known as a "sin-eater," one who helps purge the
system of its toxic effluvia, but at what price to the shaman?

The Profile of the Wounded Healer

When we examine the personal psychology of the typical
healer, we see that so often they have come from troubled
families, learning early that their "job" was to try to restore
psychological equilibrium to the family system. In his "The
Families of Origin of Social Workers," Bruce Lackie notes that
an empirical study of 1,577 professional healers, nearly three-
quarters described themselves as "the *parentified*, child, the
over-responsible member of the family, the *mediator or go-
between*, the '*good* child,' the *burden* bearer."[11]

The highest percentage of caregivers came from troubled
families of origin and "while being hypersensitive to cues and
maintaining all the qualities of a good, nondemanding
parental figure, *lack basic trust* in the world and has little faith
in his or her own ability to *stabilize* chaotic situations
significantly." Because a child really can't rebalance the
troubled world around, he or she will nevertheless carry a
chronic anxiety and feel compelled to respond over and over,
whether appropriate or not.

---

[11] Bruce Lackie, "The Families of Origin of Social Workers," 1981.
https://www.researchgate.net/publication/240339951_The_families_of_origin_
of_social_workers

Thus, he or she, are usually "wed by an overwhelming sense of *responsibility* to an intrapsychic symbiosis with his or her family." We might add that this symbiosis is naturally extended to the 'human family' in one's later life, whether one is a professional healer or not. For example, a colleague of mine on a university campus, a director of nursing, found 80% of her students came from alcohol dysfunctional families.

Lackie adds, "Good children see the kind of overt *validation* and *recognition* outside the family that their covert role within the family does not allow. They often live with considerable *guilt* despite their special position within their family." In other words, a former child, such as we all are, often operates out of a sense of shame, seemingly contaminated by the distressed world of one's origin, or out of guilt for having failed then, and most likely now, too, to fix it.

Further, Edward Hannah, in "The Relationship Between the False Self Compliance and the Motivation to Become a Professional Helper,"[12] tells us, that the "False Self (Winnicott) merges with the idea (vocation) of helper" for "during early childhood, he/she accurately perceives the he or she is needed to maintain parental narcissistic equilibrium." So, apparently, both out of the pressures of the environmental demands, as well as in service to the forlorn hope that success will then make that environment safer, and more nurturing for the child, he or she is enlisted early in a rescue mission. Moreover, "When such children become [healers], they usually have

---

[12] Edward Hannah, "The Relationship between the False Self Compliance and the Motivation to become a Professional Helper," *Smith College Studies in Social Work*, 1990. https://www.tandfonline.com/doi/abs/10.1080/00377319009516680

chronic, mostly unconscious feelings of being used as well as reactive feelings of *entitlement, rage, greed, envy,* and *contempt* … [and yet] guilt feelings in response to these reactive affects contribute to a lifelong need to make reparation for the fantasy of damaging the needed but archaic objects." Why guilt? Again, because *I failed to heal those archaic objects called Mother and Father.* Why entitlement and greed? Because I sacrificed so much of my own legitimate agenda that I am now deserving of recompense. Why envy? Because others have it easier than me. I have to carry this extra burden, invisibly. Why contempt? Because I am really above all this and wonder why they don't all just take care of their lives rather than dump it all on me.

These illogical but powerful phantasies rise from the familiar archaic thinking of the child and all of us under stress: "I am my environment. My environment is a message to me about me." In this book *Countertransference*, Gerald Searles concludes of the healer gestalt in us: "Life consists basically in his *postponement* … of his own individuation in the service of his functioning symbiotically as therapist to one or another of his family members, or to all collectively in a family symbiosis."[13]

Jung noted that virtually everyone carries and may be managed by a "pathological secret." One such secret may be expressed as the terribly haunting refrain, "I failed to heal my family." I can give you many, many examples of the depression ("learned helplessness"), anger (threat turned inward), and burnout of tired souls, tired of trying to make things work,

[13] Gerald Searles, *Countertransference and Related Subjects,* 1979.

61

and oh so tired of being tired. Learning the terrible truth that every healer must learn to survive is critical and maddening: *We cannot fix anyone, except, perhaps, perhaps, ourselves.* That day when one recognizes, as Mary Oliver wrote in "The Journey," is the day one finally leaves home, when one is determined to do

the only thing you could do —
determined to save
the only life you could save.

The Peril of Being A Wounded Healer

The continuing price of being a wounded healer is omnipresent, whether one hangs out a shingle for practice, or one stays in locked relational strategies, reflexive responses assembled years ago, and honed through repetition. These prices include:

1. *Anxiety*: Anxiety is triggered by the continuing activation of our own psychological history. (Though it did not seem funny at the time, we students in training in Zürich often felt that our first patients had all been sent to us by an omniscient Kuratorium to befuddle us because they so often presented the same problems we were wrestling with at the time). Such conversations with others naturally evokes our own complexes, the omnipresent clusters of history we carry from our past into all new relationships.

And given that those personal stories generate the affects attendant upon their generation, the wounded healer is almost always bathing in the waters of anxiety.

This anxiety activated so often leads to stress, somatic aches and pains, and either passive suffering or unconscious acting out.

Here is how the complex looks when diagrammed:

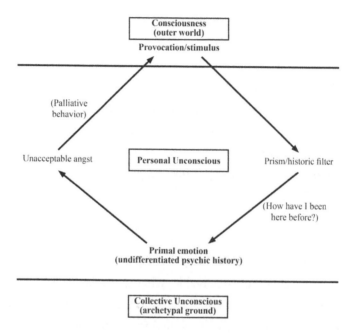

The activation of the history produces a charge of energy. The unconscious quickly sorts through the history and, via the filter of personal lens, identifies the threat. This "threat" confronts the person with one or both of the twin risks to survival: *overwhelmment* by the environment, or *abandonment* by it—either one of which can be lethal.

Along with the usual mechanism of *projection*, given that the stimulus is actually new, the second mechanism of *transference* imports the entire range of fight, flight, or freeze responses from our personal histories. Accordingly, the new situation is loaded with energy imported from our psychic basements, which accounts so often for our overcharged behaviors, which we may come to regret later. It also prejudices the new moment because it is now filed under the subject heading where our fastidious clerk at the "Office of Living History: Complex Division" placed it. Given that this circuitry takes milliseconds, we are seldom conscious of its presence until we look at the messy terrain from afar. This is how the wounded healer is fraught with anxiety at almost all times though may be wholly unaware of its interference in the conduct of daily life. This is how we live so much of the same old story so many, many times. *La plus ca change, la plus la meme chose.*

2. *Depression:*

One of the central features of depression is the feeling that its origins are irresolvable, what therapists call "learned helplessness." If one takes depression literally, it is something *pressed down* upon us. If we feel incapable of resolving it, depression is a logical expression. According to students of classical Hell, the worst part of that dismal zone was that it was forever, without resolution. That, and no room service or cable t.v., would certainly lead anyone to a number of bad days.

Given that we take in the toxins of others, allied with toxic features of our own history, our personal darkness is activated once again. And how inescapable it often feels, in particular because it catalyzes the whole archaic field of a child's powerlessness, so familiar, so persisting. Why would the evocation of learned helplessness, feeling tied to that awful place forever, not lead to depression? Only if we can consciously sever, at least for this moment, this particular arena, the linkage between the powerlessness of childhood past and the much larger powers of the mobilized adult that we are also, may we break through the depression into either action or acknowledgement of the excess baggage of the past.

3. Passivity:

Closely allied to the experience of depression is its dismal sibling called *passivity*. Therapists, most caregivers, cannot overtly solve or fix what ails the other in our purview. We confront our powerlessness over and over and so often must wait, wait, wait as opposed to our natural impulse to problem resolution. Patience is often supplanted by its distant cousin passivity, along with attendant features of guilt for not fixing the problem. For those who sit hour after hour and listen, as therapists do, the stress of those energies with nowhere to go turn inward onto the body, and all sorts of somatic features accumulate. Stiff neck, upper shoulder pain, spinal stress often receive the runoff from blocked action, contained emotion, into the body.

4. Alienation:

Still another cost of being a wounded healer, whether designated as a professional in the field or as a family member or friend, is the privacy of those moments. You know it, you face it, you suffer it, and you can't share it. In the 19th century, what we today know as therapists, were called "alienists," mostly because they dealt with folks estranged from themselves or social expectations. It is also fair to employ that word to refer to the secret-keeping that good healing often requires. When clients themselves have too often shared their therapeutic experiences with others, the accumulation of energy needed to break through an issue often bleeds out and dissipates. This work is private for more than reasons of confidentiality; it is private because the psyche has to attend the healing in its own, more effective way. The energies processing within the container have to brew and reach a catalytic pressure to produce serious change.

It is our privilege, as a professional caregiver, or even as a friend, to be invited to share the suffering of the other, and yet that adds to our own accumulating silica of suffering as well. The ancient seer Tiresias once said that sometimes we see things not meant to be seen, and yet they must be for being emotionally present, open, and available is critical to the healing dimensions of relationship. We all remember some physician or nurse or therapist or clergy who was so clinical in their attitude that we were put off by them.

To share and bear in silence is essential to healing, but it does lead the healer to feel estranged sometimes from the normal activities of life that feel so trivial, so superficial, and so ignorant of the mass of suffering all around one. I recall a colleague once saying to me, "I do this work so that someone can help me bear my loneliness." I fully understand that comment, and yet it can, and sometimes does, set the healer up for violations where the needs of the healer supersede those of the client.

There is an ancient Jewish legend of the *melamed vovnikim*, also known as "the Thirty-Six Just." The idea of the story is that no matter how bad things get on earth, God leaves 36 just souls who can hear and hold one's story of suffering. And, having been heard, the suffering soul may be assured that its story has been heard by God. It is a lovely legend. While one should never presume that one is one of those "Just," it is still a standard to which to subscribe. And, while 36 isn't enough to cover all the bases, perhaps the number is negotiable from time to time so that more of us ordinary folk can be included in that company.

The price of this alienation can lead to too much emotional separation, including repressed feeling reactions, too much isolation, too much spiral downward. Staying open to the wounds of others is critical, and yet dangerous. Still, there is a community of exiles. And it is an honor to belong to such a community.

Making Wounds Work

When asked my secret of work ethic, I often jokingly answer, "Well, mental illness works for me ..." It may not be much of a joke, for it is close to the truth. One may use one's wounds for the good of others. History is filled with examples of those who rose from their own difficult days and brought an enhanced consciousness and resolve to the common good of humankind. As Jung put it once, behind the wound often lies the genius of the person. The point of entry often becomes the point of quickened awareness as well. The key is that one is drawing on this well of experience to serve a different future, rather than just recapitulate the past, which is what will happen if one is still in the grip of the original traumata.

This is why psychoanalytic training institutes insist that the therapist undergo a long-term analysis to learn more about these blocking and causal factors in their own history. Such analysis is not a guarantee, of course, but it is a good-faith effort to be less of a problem to others. Perhaps most of all, wounds make one especially conscious around certain experiences, the addressing of which can be healing for self and other. Therefore, the traumata can, *can,* become sources of common good and enlarged meaning.

And yet, wounds can *pathologize and contaminate* the work of healing as well. So, the victim of sexual abuse may see it everywhere, and its overdiagnosis has led to some celebrated malpractice events. People in recovery have sometimes discouraged newbies from undertaking therapy at the same time, as if they were rivals for the soul of a person. More commonly, the two folks working together can fall into a joint complex, a so-called *folie a deux,* get along quite well, and yet miss the larger picture because of the gravitational pull of the common wounding experience.

But this suffering can, and mostly does, bring greater emotional and cognitive differentiation and growth to the healer. In short, we learn from our clients just as they learn from us. We learn not only what they may know in their separate life, but we learn how various paths of healing may occur and help both parties. Jung was quite emphatic that, at its heart, therapy was about two dedicated individuals working on the same existential problems. Being in the soup with someone, one is obliged to look at oneself as well.

It is always a healthy question to ask oneself, *"What would I be doing with my life without this wounding?"* Perhaps one was meant by the gods to be a tree surgeon or a country and western singer, and not to be so caught up in the now-contaminated and miasmal field of caregiving. This question can and has led some thoughtful colleagues to walk away after many years and return to a left-behind talent or enthusiasm. *What does this history make me do, and what does it keep me from doing?* These two questions have freed a lot of folks doing good work to learn that there is even better work for them in a field far away. As Jung put it, when is the good the enemy of the better?

Why Be in Helping Professions?

Among the students in Zürich at the Jung Institute in the old days, it was rumored that the question "Why do you want to become a Jungian Analyst" should never be answered by "because I want to help people." The desire to help people is not a bad thing, of course, but a deeper exploration into the question reveals that one begins because one is seeking to heal oneself. The phantasy that one might heal another is considered an inflation, a hubris, given that we all have so much healing of ourselves to do first. Helping others is a secondary phase and remains always dependent on being in right relationship to one's own soul.

When, back in the 1970s, I was asked a version of that question in an early interview of the many to come, I think I mumbled something like the work being the best way I had yet found to make sense of my own mental chaos and suffering. At that time, I had no plans to leave a comfortable world of tenured academia to attend the never-ending world of human suffering. But one of the things I learned through analysis was that some of that love of academia was my own way of avoiding how much was hurting inside me. Ivory towers, and all that. When further down the line when I was shuttling between working in a closed ward of psychotic souls in a state psychiatric hospital and a well-tailored campus, I came to realize that the conversations at the former felt more real, and went deeper, than those at the latter facility. Slowly, the shift occurred over several years, and slowly felt more and more right. While I enjoyed teaching, and still do, hence this book and others, I was backing into my true vocation after some years of ambivalence and avoidance. Vocation comes from *vocatus*, to be called. We may not wish to be called, but we all are to something, and like listening to the Daimon, it is better to respond than to flee. Artists who follow their path do not "choose" to be an artist in face of suffering, uncertainty, failure, impoverishment, and cultural marginalization, but real artists do serve the calling.

While there may be more than one vocation in the course of our lives, each one perhaps speaking to our interests, talents, situations, the call is always there, even when lost in the cacophony of outer demands, and inner urgencies. For this reason, some of my colleagues have left the work, and it was right that they answered that new call. It was not burnout but rather the stirrings of the soul seeking new seas to sail.

So, the concomitant question naturally rises: How does the wounded healer address self-healing? I am glad you asked that question.

Self-Treatment

Just as Nietzsche once asked, who will teach the teacher, we are brought back to this question: Who will heal the healer? Here are some thoughts along those lines for you to consider.

Not surprisingly, I favor each person who so wishes to engage in a personal therapy, including from time to time therapists also. Remember that the etymology of the word *therapy* means to listen to, pay attention to, attend, serve. Psychotherapy, then, would be attending to, serving your own soul—what could be so bad about that? The basic purpose of therapy is to engage in an ongoing dialogue around the meaning of one's journey, asking such questions as:

1. What are my patterns, especially the self-defeating choices? What "complexes," clusters of energy in my history, create those patterns? What do they make me do and keep me from doing?
2. What has always pulled at my sleeve, asked recognition from me, and even now wishes to be honored and lived in the world? What wishes to enter the world through me, rather than what does the world want from me?

Of course, a formal therapy is not required or appropriate for everyone. And it is sometimes hard to find a therapist these days who has lived the journey and therefore can go to those depths with you. But, and this is an important but, one still has to ask these questions of oneself. Sometimes it is useful to bounce them off another and get a response that helps us see outside our frame, but when that is not possible, at least asking large questions of ourselves will lead to a larger life than when left to routinization and a government by complexes.

One thing I noted of the analysts with whom I worked in Zürich was that they, wise elders, had lived their lives, with all its vicissitudes, were not glib or naïve or formulaic. They also lived their lives with passion. Remembering that *passio* is the Latin for "suffering," it means engaging in something which one feels so much that it hurts, but which, in engaging, much meaning is experienced. Most of them also had alternative interests: gardening, art, music, sculpting, sport, and the like. They were curious, multidimensional, and had a life outside their work. As Jung noted, one cannot take a client further than one has traveled oneself. Thus, they had to have a life before they could look at the life of another with a measure of distance and engagement and passion.

Any wounded healer has also to continue to re-vision the journey, not only through therapy, but meditation, active imagination, dreamwork, bodywork, and continued study and reflection on the meaning of our immersion in the vast ocean of mystery in which we swim. Curiosity is our best guide, along with an open mind, and an open heart for discovery.

Any wounded healer, therapist, or any of us, must develop rituals of *"emptying" or "washing clean."* If we absorb toxic material in our work, in our relationships, what heals us, what frees us? I think each person must find a life outside the work through sport, bodywork, mediation, music or whatever brings another part of the psyche to the center and thus compensates for the worry and stress of the work. At the end of the day, I never read a work of psychology, *per se*, but rather history and occasionally spy novels. One can learn a lot by "getting away," and what one learns brings one back to the work in a refreshed and more informed way.

Ultimately, any "healer," will survive only with a recognition of one's limits, and the limits of our various "sciences." The 12 Step folks and the Buddhists have been there ahead of many of us. The former group say, "Let go, and let God," which is a way of saying, "You can't fix this. Stop going crazy thinking you can. This work belongs to a pay grade several levels above you."

And the Buddhists have for millennia reminded us that the chief cause of human suffering rises from the ego's phantasy of sovereignty. The more it wishes control, the more life evades its program. The recent pandemic is a perfect example of this delusion. The best systems in the world failed, often complicated by human pathology, but underneath all of this is the terrible majesty of nature doing its thing. Thus Buddhism has urged us not to push the river, but to go with it, and seek to live in as much harmony with the Tao of nature as is possible.

Finally, and perhaps most important of all, one must recover, or re-member, a participation in the grand mystery of it all. We are here a short while, and while imbued with large longings, we are equipped with finite tools. The more we simply sit back and puzzle, look at the stars above, or the vast constellations whirling within each of us, and enjoy the view, our brief moment in this infinite pageant before us and after us, the more we feel fully here.

The wounded healer brings much good to this world. But our powers are so profoundly limited. Running from this summons is a flight from life itself, and an overidentification with its work is a pathology of its own. How to attend the suffering of the other, hold to one's own agenda of growth and witness, is a continuing challenge. The wounded healer in each of us is asking each of us to attend this work more consciously, more vigorously, but it also wishes us to have more compassion for the parts in us that hurt so much. If we forget them, we aren't going to be very much good for others either.

Chapter Four
On the Psychology of Comedy:
Is the Joke on Us?

"The secret source of humor is not joy but sorrow, and there is no humor in heaven."

Mark Twain

"Swallow a toad in the morning and you will encounter nothing more disgusting the rest of the day."

Nicolas Chamfort

A funny thing happened on the way to the grave. After the dread, the weeping, the grieving, someone laughed. (I once had an older lady client who frequently said to me, "Honey, I'm so old, I don't even buy green bananas these days.") It's the craziest of paradoxes: This animal that we are has consciousness through which we may bring so many gifts and curses into the world, and yet the ultimate gift/curse of consciousness is to be aware of one's transient nature, our headlong flight toward annihilation. As Horace Walpole said, "Life is a tragedy to those who feel, and a comedy to those who think." So, go figure.

But let me start with a story. Two humans are eating another. Not a very appetizing story, right? But if I say, two cannibals are eating a clown, we move into different territory. And when one of them pauses and says, "Hey, taste something funny here?" we now have a joke. What just happened? At first you felt a *frisson*, a brief shudder at the image, a whiff of anxiety, and then the paradox at what is being eaten: Oh, a *clown*. Something "funny," and the tension is broken, and even the horrific is resolved, leveled, brought back down to the acceptable. And the release of that tension is the laugh that rises from our bodies.

Now some of you weren't laughing at that joke, I can see. Much like my wife, whom I daily oppress by telling jokes: dad jokes, bad jokes, meta-jokes, and the lot. The worse the better. She once said, "Relationship is having one special person to annoy for a very long time." I think she was joking, but if not, I try to annoy her every day with a joke or two. "Meta-joke," you ask? Well, a priest, a rabbi, and a minister walk into a bar, and the bartender says, "Hey, is this some kind of joke or something?" (You are free to laugh now, or not). It is a *meta-joke* because the tension raised is between the setup described, and a long tradition of jokes, especially merging the subgenres of bar jokes and clergy jokes. The barroom is the scene in which the *meta* (Greek: over, beyond, across) bridges the genres, links the quotidian with the transcendent. So, the tension is broken by the bartender who allows the two frames to be reconciled, and then released, through laughter. (You may laugh now).

Is comedy a variant of tragedy, as Twain seems to suggest? Three elderly chaps are talking about their last wishes on their deathbeds. The first says, "For my last wish, I want all my family there so we can be together at the end." The second says, "For my last wish, I want the entire nation to mourn my absence." The third says, "For my last wish, I want someone to approach the coffin and say, 'Hey, look! He's still moving...'" Robert Frost pondered the ironies of our existential absurdities and wrote in a wry couplet, "Forgive O Lord my little joke on thee, / And I'll forgive Thy great big joke on me." Reportedly, Oscar Wilde's last remarks were, "Either that wallpaper has to go, or I do." If he didn't say it, it is Wildean enough to be true.

From whence cometh the ideas of *comedy*, and *tragedy*, and *humor*, you ask? Well, comedy comes from the Greek *kome* which means "village." So, comedy, as in Dante's Divine thingee, means "of the village," namely in the vulgar tongue, ribald, and direct from and to where people really live. Tragedy comes from the Greek for the "goat-song," rising out of the periodic ceremonies in honor of the dying/reborn god Dionysius. (Since this essay is not about tragedy, we won't go there this time). Humor comes from the medieval/Renaissance physiological notion of human character and personality typology rising from the relative mixtures of the four fluids called "humors." So, Ben Jonson's 1598 *Every Man in His Humor* depicts the comic examples of personality types arising out of the prevalence of these humors: Too much black bile produces melancholy or depression; yellow bile produces biliousness, a constricted personality; red bile produces choler, or anger; and phlegm produces a phlegmatic, or lethargic, individual. This typology lasted for many decades, even centuries, and helped explain our sundry orientations to the world and our various mood states.

Similarly, the archetypal image of the Fool is a recognition of the need for some energy to upset the apple cart, to be the carrier of the counterculture values of any era. The fool in Shakespeare, and elsewhere, is usually the only one who can get away with telling the compensatory truth. So, Lear's fool essentially tells Lear who the fool in the kingdom is, the one who does not know the difference between narcissistic hunger and love, and he gets away with it because he is the fool. Related to the fool is the Trickster archetype. Found in every culture, he is the one who makes sure things don't get too formulaic, too predictable. He makes us forget our car keys when we think we are in charge of life. He reminds, too late, of course, that the devil is in the details. All of these energies, these embodiments as archetypal characters serve to remind us of the power of comedy to bring inflated things down to their humble human place. However important we think we are, the gods have hidden a banana peel out there, waiting, just for us.

As we get serious about laughing, let me present seven ideas on how comedy works on us, socially and psychologically.

1. The general function of our comedic capacity is to be able to hold the tensions of our experience for a moment and to safely release those tensions through the expulsion of emotion known as laughter. Alternatively, we might just as soon release that tension through a primal scream. We have Aristotle's notes on his lectures on tragedy wherein he describes the salubrious effect that occurs when one releases re-

pressed affect that otherwise might breed pathologies. The capacity of the audience to identify with the suffering of the protagonist and, at the same time, experience through the aesthetic event a catharsis, a purgation of toxic affect is part of our psyche's self-regulating system.

Similar to the tragic vision, the comic vision feasts on the trauma, privation, fear, and ultimate annihilation of human life. (The comedic release of tension was probably also addressed by Aristotle, but we have lost that work). But tragedy and comedy are rightly parallel images of the theater because both express our wonder and horror at the dilemmas of human experience and our possible release of the tension through an expulsion of affect. After this purgation, we feel better ... somewhat.

A Scottish researcher tracked the neurological effect of comedy and indicated that the experience of laughter involves a number of complex interactions. And folks with damage to the frontal right hemispheres of the brain do not find jokes funny. (Be warned now, if you don't like the jokes in this essay).

   2. The comic sensibility helps us reframe our experience, see our lives in different ways. Some amazing humor has come out of those living in COVID sequestering. Laughter is not only a coping mechanism and emotional release, it helps see one's life from a different perspective.

So, a guy goes to the doctor and says, "When I touch my head, it hurts. When I touch my knee, it hurts. When I touch my back, it hurts." The doctor gives him an examination and says, "I know what your problem is, you have a broken finger!" Sometimes humor helps us see our world from another angle and, in so doing, broadens all things. So, this guy is lost in the desert. Finally, at the end of his reserve, he sees a roadside stand. He thinks he can get some water there, but it is only selling ties. He screams at the vendor about needing water, not a tie. He crawls on and now is wholly spent, and then he comes to this beautiful oasis with fountains gushing with water. As he approaches the gate of entrance, down to his last ounce of energy, the guard within says, "I'm sorry, sir, but you have to have a tie to get in here."

3. Comedy helps mediate the disjunctions of life, a world in which the absurd reigns, catch-22 prevails, and Murphy's Law is upheld by the highest courts in the land. A guy goes to pick up his car and asks if the brakes were fixed. The mechanic says, "Sorry, we couldn't do that, but we made your horn louder." And then there is the lady who rushed into her OB/GYN and says, "Doctor, doctor, I think I am shrinking." "It's OK," her doctor says, "you just have to be a little patient." A Valley Girl goes into a California library and says very loudly, "I'd like a Big Mac and cheese." "Sssshhhh," says the lady at the counter, "this is a library!" "OK," the Valley Girl whispers, "can I have fries with that?" (*Ta dum…*).

4. Comedy often deflates *hybris*, reminds one of the elemental limits of our human condition. Steven Wright said that he planned to live forever, "So far, so good." The classic pratfall is the arrogant person in the top hat slipping on the banana peel, some kin to the

one that waits out there for each of us. Hybris brought low, the leveling of nature achieved. This image was treated most seriously by theologians past who called it, naturally, "the Fall." A lady asks the doctor if her case is serious, and he says, "I am afraid so, ma'am." "I'd like a second opinion," she retorts. "Well … I think you're ugly, too," he said. Whenever the human gets too high, the gods observe, enact the law of *enantiodromia*, and the Fall is forthcoming. The local hot shot brags at how he quickly solved the puzzle in less than a month, especially since it announced "3-5 years" on the carton.

5. Comedy so often depends on the metaphoric tool we possess to help us stand in relationship to the inexplicable, such as the gods, or how the high and the low are really aspects of the same thing. Through metaphor we are able to discern the secret relationships that connect disparate things. So, Billy Collins writes a paean to his dog Dharma in a poem of the same name and talks of his utter faithfulness, his modest cost, and his few needs. While he ends by praising Dharma for his many gifts of devotion, but all is balanced daily by reprehensibly snitching the cat's food and treating the poet as a God.

6. Comedy also sometimes helps us express the inexpressible, the forbidden, the repressed. Jung, who was known for his deep laugh and great sense of humor, never wrote about comedy. In 1905, dour Freud wrote his book *Jokes and Their Relationship to the Unconscious*. In that work he noted how often humor could be savage, biting, bigoted, lascivious, and

the like—all leakages from repression, all expressions of the forbidden. Like dreams, jokes employed the mechanisms of compression, displacement, double entendre, and so on. Like dreams, jokes facilitate the forbidden, the repressed to have its say, and thereby perhaps are less pathogenic than the monsters of repressed affect. William Blake the 19th-century poet noted the cost of repression, saying hyperbolically: "Sooner murder an infant in its cradle than nurse unacted desires."

Jokes can be obscene, smutty, sexist, and if someone takes offense, the joke is on them because they can't take a joke. When I was a college student, I was privileged to have a roommate from Korea, my "Seoul mate," I called him. One day someone said they had to go to the john, and Young Bae had just learned that another student was named John. He put them together and fell on the floor laughing. He couldn't believe a parent would name their child "Toilet" in any language. Actually, that's an old joke. In *Troilus and Cressida*, Shakespeare—whose audience was variously referred to as the "groundlings" and "the penny stinkards"—has the Greek hero Ajax frequently referred to as *A-Jakes*. Yes, going to the Jake was the same then. A real Elizabethan knee-slapper, that!

One of the beauties of New Jersey is that its citizens have enough sense of self, and sense of humor, to laugh at themselves, unlike some other areas of the country I could name. (You know who you are, Lone Star). "So how many union guys from Newark are needed to change that light bulb?" "Twelve. Ya gotta problem with that?" OK, Texas, you get one also. Two coeds sit next to each other on a Southwest flight from HOU to DCA. The Houston gal, being friendly, says, "So, where y'all from?" The Easterner replies, "From a place where we don't end our sentences with prepositions." The Houston gal thinks awhile, and then says, "So, where y'all from, bitch"? I once received a card with two Freudian types passing each other: "Hello…." "Hello…." Inside, we see each one thinking, "I wonder what he meant by that?" Or how many Jungians does it take to drive to the Jung Society lectures? Two: one to drive, one to point out where the driver missed the turnoff. (Thank you, David).

Comics from Lenny Bruce to Richard Pryor to Chris Rock to Trevor Noah can skewer the bastions of racism. Sexism, too, becomes, laughable. Dave Barry observes that "there are two theories about arguing with women. Neither works." And comediennes have retorted, "What does it mean when a man is in your bed gasping for breath and calling your name? You didn't hold the pillow down long enough!" And "Why does it take 100 million sperm to fertilize one egg? Because not one will stop and ask for directions."

It can address the vegetal and scatological as well. My friend Martin in London told me about the time when Sir Winston was in the privy when an official with the title Lord Privy Seal visited him in an officious and annoying way and demanded an immediate audience. Churchill boomed out, "Tell the Lord Privy Seal that I am sealed in the privy and can deal with only one shit at a time."

We all know that mimicry and satire can be a very penetrating means of scoring points. Many editorial cartoons depend on humor to scour the opposition. Being laughed at is the best treatment possible for the inflated, the self-important.

    7. Comedy can also embody a flickering of the human spirit in the darkest of hours. A number of years ago I read an encyclopedia of Jewish humor, and yes, there was one whole chapter on concentration camp humor. How dimly the spirit must have flickered there, but it was never extinguished. During the Nazi occupation of Holland, food was terribly scarce. A soldier occupier asks a Dutch farmer, "What do you feed your horse," hoping to trap him into revealing a secret cache of corn or oats. The farmer replies, "I just give him a couple of guilders, and he goes out and gets what he wants."

Satire, irony, puns, and parody are comedic modes with critical capacities and can often serve as very effective tools of criticism. Jonathan Swift got away with a great deal when he took on the repressive policies of the British Empire in Ireland by writing his rationally savage "A Modest Proposal," in which he suggested that England's economically rapacious appetite and Irish poverty could be reconciled if the Irish sold their babies as food exports. (One wonders if that might be where we got the terms "peasant under glass" or how poor kids get into good families. Sorry).

Ultimately, satire, irony, and parody can democratize, bring the inflated down to a proper level, deflate the powerful, and remind them all of their limits. As one French wit observed, tyrants can defeat opposing armies but can never defeat raillery and ridicule. What potentates are really able to posture in such a frightening way when they are laughed at? If the Germans could have laughed at Hitler's posturing or

Mussolini's outthrust chin, so many more of us would have lived. Who can forget the gorgeous Brits who welcomed the president of the United States with a blimp of Baby Trump? *Wit*, by the way, comes from the German *wissen*, (*Weisheit*—wisdom) "to know." So, a wit is usually a learned person who with humor or biting satire can make a pointed remark that has wisdom to it.

And puns ... well, I am hesitant. The esteemed Dr. Samuel Johnson once said, "He who would make a pun would as lief cut a purse." That's a serious threat. A cut-purse was a thief who cut someone's bag of coins from their belt, the punishment for which was hanging at Tyburn Hill, the place of execution. So, you can understand my reluctance. And all I wanted with the good Doctor was to have some pun. But my anxiety diminished after a clown opened a door for me and I thought, "That is a really nice Jester."

One of the paradoxes of puns is that they require an imaginative leap, a sometimes brilliant bridging of opposites, and often eventuate in a groan as the labor in making this connection is revealed. When modern poet Alan Tate writes, "We are the eyelids of defeated caves," we do not groan, but we struggle to figure out where he is going. His line works in a poem, bridging the immense gap between images—what in the 17th century "metaphysical poets" was a construction called "conceits"—but the poor pun ends in ridicule. But both mediate the immense opposites, link the disparate, and reveal a secret unity underneath.

So surely, comedy must serve some valuable function in our psycho-spiritual life. The need to puncture pretension, to level the inflated, to remind any of us of our limits, is to serve an acknowledgement that occasionally the human ego needs to be brought back into a more respectful relationship with the Tao of things. The joke *is* always on us, and when we are impressed with our own magnificence, that is one of our best sources of remembering what is important to remember.

There is an old legend that the *Book of Life* has alternating pages of tragedy and comedy. On one occasion, the book was reportedly found, and the reader was observed to be hurrying through the pages to see what the final word would prove to be. When he reached the final page, he bent over, his face a rictus of reaction, tears running down his face, and observers couldn't tell whether he was laughing or crying.

We have to remember that below our shiny surface is a skeleton, yet I think among the 200-plus bones there is one called the funny bone. The funniest person I ever met was my son, Tim. Along with his many parodies of his father's work, he used to warn me to be nice to him because he would be the one picking out my nursing home. Similarly, I should be nice because he would be the one to decide when to pull the plug. I hastened to caution him that having a really bad cold, or even a bad hair day, did not qualify as one of those terminal indications. The real joke turned out to be that I would be the one placing his ashes on a hill overlooking Santa Fe. Go figure …

So, OK, one more. A guy brings a dog into a bar and says to the bartender, "I have a talking dog." "Nah…" says the bartender. "Yes, ask it a question and if he is right, give me a beer." "OK," the bartender says pointing downward, "that is the floor; what is that up there?" The dog looks awhile and says, "rooouuff, rooouuff." "Come on, you phony," the bartender yells. "Try one more," the man says. "OK, who was the greatest baseball player of all time?" The dog thinks a moment and says, "ruuufff, ruuff." The bartender throws them both out into the street. The dog walks over to its master and says, "I should have said DiMaggio?"

Chapter Five
Permutations of Desire

"A neurosis is an offended god."

C. G. Jung

"The fire of the gods drives us to set forth by day
And by night. So, come, let us look at what is apparent,
And seek what is ours, as distant as it may be!"
Friedrich Hölderlin, "Bread and Wine"

Recently I sat in therapy with a business consultant who felt she had crossed a professional boundary with her client, another woman somewhat her junior. This latter person spoke of how she was living in a loveless, sexless relationship with a person who had considerable difficulties with commitment and carry-through. They had not made love for several months. My client reported how she urged the younger woman to leave the present unhappiness and reconnect with a man whom she knew she loved and whom she knew loved her. "I was ashamed to tell her that I once lived in a sexless marriage for 30 years, but I knew that I could not stand by and watch her live the same kind of life." She wondered what possessed her to jump into her client's personal life even as she saw her younger self about to make the mistake she had made decades earlier.

Before we think this is all about sex, we need to remember that sometimes sex is not about sex—even though it also always is, even when it is not. My client is reporting what a significant number of clients have reported to me in recent years. Many of them were trained to believe that sex is not that important, that they need to be dutiful in the face of commitments, and that the fault is no doubt somehow theirs. What we are talking about here are what we might call "disorders of desire." While levels of desire vary from person to person, the absence or diminution of desire is psychologically and spiritually significant for it is desire that most expresses the life force. If we find other elemental functions troubled, eating and sleeping for example, then we take them seriously from a clinical perspective. Surely, we remember that the classical imagination regarded Eros as a god, variously described as the oldest of the gods for providing the fundament of being itself and the youngest as he renews in every instant. Pallid portraits of an effete Cupid, he of the drooping diaper, are hardly up to the raw powers of desire, even though one is reminded that all arrows hurt when they are embedded in one's own flesh.

Freud, of course, returned us, and our age, to a deepened consideration of how desire drives us. We are, indisputably, pleasure-seeking, pain-avoiding animals. When primary desires are blocked, or closely guarded by cultural sanctions, desire goes underground into the body, into projections, into vicarious sublimations. But, as Jung thoughtfully added, we are also the symbol-making animal, and these permutations of desire constitute the rich differentiations of the soul (*psyche*) as well as body (*soma*). In his epochal *Symbols of Transformation*, published in 1912, Jung demonstrated how libido is more than biological drive; it is the propellent power for our psychospiritual development, the permutations of which provide the vast spectrum of our cultural forms. (Think of the imaginative expression of the celibate Victorian priest Gerard Manley Hopkins in his, "That Nature is a Heraclitean Power and the Comfort of the Resurrection.") So, is lusting for one's neighbor's warm embrace no different from lusting for communion with God? Ask John Donne, who wrote the most erotic poems of divine worship, or Teresa of Avila, whom Gian Lorenzo Bernini depicts in transports of orgasmic ecstasy. Or recall Blake, who asked:

> What is it men in women do require?
> The lineaments of Gratified Desire.
> What is it women do in men require?
> The lineaments of Gratified Desire.

Buried in the etymologies of our words lie primal perceptions, radical engagements with wonder, and with terrifying mystery. In encountering the numinosity of Zeus, one experiences the radical amazement of "lightening." It is not that Zeus is a solar deity, but that the wonder of encountering his power overwhelms conscious categories, not unlike standing in the darkness and being flooded by the dawn's thunderous appearance out of blackness, a "lightening" experience. So, the etymology of *desire* derives from the Latin *desiderare*, "to long for," derived from *de sidere*, "of the stars." Thus, disorders of desire arise from our loss of the stars, namely, some sidereal point from which our course may be derived and our voyage charted. As mariners on the sea of Eros, we all need that star to guide us lest we fall adrift and prey to monsters of the deep—variously named Depression, Despair, Desuetude—which can so casually devour us.

From the Old English we gain *lust*: "desire and pleasure"; and the German *lust*, "desire," and *lustig*, comical, and then *lascivious*, wanton and lustful; and *cupidity*, which is lustful, especially in regard to wealth, and derives from the Latin *cupido*, "desire." (Think of the fusion of the two in the erotic song "Money," between the seedy nightclub impresario and Sally Bowles in "Cabaret.") Similarly, the worship of the goddess Venus becomes *venery* and *venereal* and also begets *concupiscence*. (St. Augustine prays to be relieved of his concupiscence, "but not just yet," he adds. Apparently, he was painfully caught between competing deities. Early church Father Origen castrates himself, thinking that the severed organ will no longer think *through* him, although imagination has no organ limitation and quickly renews its compelling and confounding summons to his imagination). Occasionally, the worship of the goddess Venus becomes *venery*, a sport in which it is rather easy to earn a scarlet letter.

From the French *appetence*: desire, we get *appetite*. And from the Greek *an*: without, and *orexis*: appetite, desire, we get that disorder of desire we call *anorexia*. So, what, in times of relative plenty, leads to the loss of desire? In *Notes From the Underground* (1863), the first great work of depth psychology, Fyodor Dostoevski argues that the heart and soul of the modern is slowly being stifled by our separation from instincts (the death of Pan) resulting from our deracination from nature through urbanization, the experience of anonymity, (*vide* Franz Kafka's "The Metamorphosis," a portrait of radical depersonalization), and our submission to mass ideologies such as "progress," which confuse meaning with material comforts. In such a world, the Underground Man notes, we have only the perversity of our eros, the power to stick our tongue out at the prevailing, dominating values, and to prove every day that we are not as programmed as piano keys to hit the same chord with every stroke.

Why are there so many passionless lives, so many banal and loveless relationships, and why do we carry so many unsurfeited hearts with us as we journey toward the final darkness? We are the sum of our stories, and yet something more. I recall recently speaking with another person who is living in a passionless marriage and passionless life: "Both you and your husband are living your scripts sincerely, both of you. He accepted his male story that he was to be successful—make money, live in the 'burbs, buy you baubles, procreate your kind through at least two children. You have lived yours—marry 'successfully,' procreate your kind, do charitable works, and it will all go where it is supposed to go. Why, then, are you having an affair, and why is he so desolate after getting the promotion he fought for all these years"? Beneath his conscious life, something deeper knows and finds these trophies empty; beneath her conscious life, something deeper knows and finds these achievements empty. Each has sought a "successful" life, each has achieved everything he or she sought, and both find themselves without passion.

When Jung defined neurosis as suffering that has not yet found its meaning, he was describing this set of good people. Each suffers the absence of authenticity and is haunted from below by the anguish of a life unlived. Desire is not served when it is stunted, thwarted, or deflected to trivializing ends. This story will not end well, or easily. They will stay together and lead trivialized lives; or they will separate and pursue other wills-o-the-wisps. Or perhaps, one or both may yet come to consciousness and risk leading a larger, more dangerous life. After all, *passio* is the Latin word for suffering—which form of suffering is all that lies within our hands. Either way, we get suffering.

Clearly, there are other stories also moving through us, invisible energy streams that drive and shape our histories: genetic stories, archetypal stories, and internalized messages from our fortuitous histories, better known as *complexes*. We have complexes because we have histories, and these charged shards of internalized experience, replete with bodily manifestation (a flush of nausea, sweating palms, constricted throat); a rush of energy that piles on the present moment the monstrous enormity of the past; an archaically ground lens through which the new may only be seen through the perspective of the old; and an attendant script, with splinter personalities, driving the reenactment of mythologemes with replicative outcomes.

The word *paraphilias* in our time refers to the various sexual disorders as identified by the American Psychiatric Association. Given that sex is not always about sex, let us consider that etymology as well and see it as a parabolic expression of love (*philos*) which, driven by desire, finds its expressions through various symbolic avenues. Why, in the most abundant civilization in history, do we have so many eating disorders? Why, amid our surfeited world of elemental needs long met, is our prevailing mythos, ideology, and pathology *materialism*? Why is this materialism the most seductive religion in the world? Do we ever pause before the refrigerator or the purchase at the mall and say, "That which I am seeking I will not find here," or are we driven by the power of a deeper desire? What *mater*, the archetype of nurturance, then, do we really seek?

What is coursing within us, what drives such compelling desire? When we recall that we begin this perilous journey with a primal, traumatic separation from the Other, an estrangement from which we never wholly recover, we realize in part why we might spend our lives seeking to restore such a connection. The inordinate investment in the idea of "romance" is one such compensatory agenda, as is the search for reconnection with "God," as the etymology of religion suggests (*re-legare*). During this brief transit we possess two gifts—consciousness of the gift of life and consciousness of its short loan from party or parties unknown. We owe two gifts in return—a life fully lived and a life surrendered at the end. As that great American philosopher, the Sage of Tupelo, MS, said, "Return to sender. / Address unknown. / No such number. / No such phone." (For the younger among you, that is Elvis, who has reportedly left the building).

Such disconnects are experienced by individuals and by cultures when they are separated from their mythological roots. When one feels linked to the ancestors, or to the gods, or to the natural world, one feels at home, one's terror of extinction is subsumed in the great round of return to origins, but when one has suffered the erosion of those linkages, then one feels even more the cold breath of eternal night, and the urgency of those transient and momentary solaces of putative paraphilic connections—whatever form they take. When Rilke reflected on this matter he concluded in his third *Duino Elegy* that we all carry, all perpetuate, all pass on an ancestral longing to connect to the Other, an endless desire-driven urgency because "… we do not live, as the flowers, for a single year. For, through us, an immortal sap rises through our limbs."

It may be of interest to the reader that in psychiatric circles our old friend and frequent companion, "depression," has by and large departed, replaced by something called "dysthymic disorder." *Thymos* is the Greek word for strong feeling. Accordingly, a depressed person is not, apparently, going to have a strong feeling for life. (I do love how even the psychiatric manuals fall into metaphor when describing these moments). Even though it runs against the grain of the contemporary temper to suffer, from a psychodynamic perspective we do not immediately seek the removal of the symptom. We know that the symptom is actually a message from the depths, namely, an autonomous reaction by our psyche as to how our life is going, when viewed from its transcendent perspective. Even though we may have consciously served all the values, complexes, marching orders our time and place presented us, we may still suffer depression. What, then, is "pressed down," what is seeking a larger expression from below? These most obvious questions are the last the souls of our era ask.

How radical it is, and how profound it may prove, to ask rather: *What does psyche want from me?* This is not a question we have ever been equipped to ask, and will not ask, until psyche drives us to our knees. Then we may discover that the energy that desire embodies has not gone away; *it has gone somewhere else.* Where is it, and how do we track it, and how do we bring it back to serve conscious life? These are the questions that the shamans of tribal life addressed more consciously than our aggregated armamentaria of medications and behavioral modifications have managed.

Repeatedly, I have seen that many need to recover an elemental permission to be who they are, desire what they desire, and live what life is asking of them. What are they waiting for—permission from someone? An extra century to piddle around? How tentatively we all act. How did our species arrive here without enlisting in the derby of desire that so often created a new age: the desire to fly, the desire to explore, the desire to create? There may have been thousands of reasons these things were not permitted, but desire won out, and our world grew apace. Without desire, life sickens, and the demon of lethargy triumphs.

As W. H. Auden lamented in his poem "In Memory of Sigmund Freud,"

Over his grave
the household of Impulse mourns one dearly loved:
sad is Eros, builder of cities,
and weeping anarchic Aphrodite.

When we track that energy to its lair, and honor the dishonored god it represents, then we find we are once again driven by declensions of desire, and are in service to life.

Chapter Six
All Is Fire: the Imagination as Aperture into Psyche

"The imagination lends to airy nothing a local habitation and a name."

W. Shakespeare

"Perhaps creating something is nothing but an act of profound remembrance."

R. M. Rilke

Pre-Socratic philosopher Heraclitus once observed that "all is fire," a lambent metaphor for the flickering, energetic transformation of material forms: creating, disassembling, devouring itself, process personified. From the archaic realms of imagination to the discoveries of quantum physics, we intuit what dismays our senses—that nothing is substantial— below *Dinglichkeit*, "thingness," materiality, floats no-thingness. All phenomena, (*natura naturans*, nature naturing), appear to such epiphenomena as mind, sensibility, consciousness, as stable, fixed, and objectified. But all things are transforming, composing and decomposing, even as the human ego, that most fragile barque of all, tossing on tenebrous seas, would fix them, hold them, control them. Every appearance to our sensibility is an instant only, a snapshot of the already-disappearing, or as Apollinaire's *"Cors de Chaisse"* reminds, history is a hunting horn whose sound dies out along the wind. Or G. M. Hopkins's nomination that nature is a Heraclitean fire. Or Rilke's glimpse of the gods in passing, always passing, *"nur ein Spur,"* only a trace, and then the no-thingness. *Natura naturans* quickly becoming *nature naturata*, nature naturing cum nature natured.

And for all the transience of material forms, how much more insubstantial the *psyche*, that strange word we translate as *soul* but which has wind, breathing, and transformation from pupae into butterfly in its etymological ancestry. So it is, the most fleeting is apprehended by, perceived by, construed, animated, turned, torqued and tortured by us—by something still more fleeting. As Rilke notes in his ninth *Duino Elegy*, this evanescent world is rendered conscious by us, "the most fleeting of all," this *Sein-zum-Tode*, spinning toward its imminent dissolution, death, dismemberment, and decay. So the world is lent a local habitation and a name by this creature whose sand is always running through the glass, and as G. M. Hopkins notes, sand, at first seeming "at the wall fast / but mined with a motion that crowds and combs to a fall."

When David Hume, Immanual Kant, and others declared that we cannot know the *Thing* in its thingness, but only our experience of the thing, metaphysics died, perhaps much theology, too, and obliged the birth of phenomenology and depth psychology. Phenomenology studies the conditions of experience, its limitations and capacities, and refrains from absolute pronouncements lest it be bewitched by its own legerdemain as so much theology, political rhetoric, and sloganeering has succumbed. Without a sustained, disciplined analysis of the conditions of, and limitations, of experience, we slip into the oldest of semantic and delusional heresies: idolatry. We mistake our constructs, our metaphors, our fictive intimations for the thing itself and thus become servant to our construings rather than sustaining a radical openness to mystery. So, the image, the trace, *ein Spur*, left behind by the passing god, is worshipped, deified, reified, while the departed divinity is already elsewhere. And how many have died in the name of ossified metaphors? How many tortured by the literalism of the single-minded. "O Lord us keep," as Blake petitioned, "from Single Vision, and from Newton's sleep."

Depth psychology, too, is tasked with the formidable: to bring us into relationship with the invisible world, to track its peregrinations and permutations of the unconscious, and to render conscious what is unconscious. The problem with the unconscious is that it is unconscious, and therefore we can say nothing about it definitively. We project that it exists because of several daily facts: "Stuff" keeps spilling into our world without our intending them; we experience multiple autonomous phenomena that are clearly emanating from us: patterns, dreams, symptoms; and sooner or later, we are challenged by the world's abrasive reminders to account for our presence and apparent choices, and the wake of consequences we leave behind us.

We can only gain momentary purchase on that invisible realm when psyche informs image in matter, in mind, in imagination that, as noted in *A Mid-Summer Night's Dream*, "Lends to airy nothing a local habitation and a name". Newton could track the informing of matter and derive from it "laws," which allow us to weigh, shape, direct, predict, and control the movement of matter. In so doing, he believed he was reading the mind of God in an act of piety. If he had thought that others would drop the hypothesis of the Divine and run with those "laws," he might have had second thoughts. (When Napoleon a century and a half later asked Pierre-Simon LaPlace where God was in his cosmic scheme, the mathematician replied that he no longer needed that hypothesis). That high school physics classes currently employ theses and concepts that transcend Newton's imaginal scheme in no way obviates his aesthetic vision of an ordered universe; it simply means we have better instruments, better questions today, and can imagine more.

Today the depth psychological enterprise is to track the movement of the invisible as it manifests in the venues of mind, body, patterns, neurology, dreams, and the like. That so few psychologists address the interaction with the un-conscious is a failure of nerve to take on the really difficult dialogue. Even so, the task for the behaviorist, cognitive therapist, psychiatrist or psychoanalyst is the same: to track the movement of the invisible, swirling energies by *attending the image* that is currently animated by their ostensible presence. The ineluctable passages of the gods, their rise, immanence, relocation elsewhere, the investments in the body of repressed affect, or the dreams that trouble sleep—all are the traces that the depth psychologist must track in order to discern their infections, blockages, misdirected vectors, and ultimate agendas. It is the sum of these movements, these passages, arrivals and departures, which constitute our personal biographies and collectively add chips to history's mosaic. The more we are able to follow these breadcrumbs through the forests of the soul, the more we enhance consciousness, that fragile atoll in a foam-wracked, sometimes engulfing, sea.

A little over a century ago, C. G. Jung published an epochal book that almost nobody reads today except my students. Originally titled *Wandlungen und Symbole der Libido, Transformations and Symbols of Libido*, it is better known today in its subsequent editions as *Symbols of Transformation*. Jung used the term *libido* because it was the currency of the hour, a term he quickly redefines and by so doing splits himself off from Freud forever. While Freud had taken this old Latin word *libido* and used it to provide an energic schema of the psyche in its many functions, he limited its use to the biological drives, frustrations, and secondary elaborations that this vast river coursing through the body takes in seeking both solace and satiety. Adler, Jung noted, had usefully reminded us that we are also social animals and that a good deal of daily dynamics arises from the inter-active dramas of family life and social setting. To this, Jung added his understanding of libido that the elemental life force is, of course, biologically driven, socially shaped, and yet, even more, reflects a central yet epiphenomenal curiosity that this particular animal craves, longs for, suffers the loss of, and is driven by the search for meaning. We are, Jung reminded us, symbol-making animals and through the tools of metaphor, symbol, and picture-making, we seek to stand in some sort of conscious relationship to the *Mysterium*, which our universe embodies for us. These tools do their work through analogue.

Knowing that we cannot know the things in themselves, we approach them through things more commonly experienced. We understand Robert Burns immediately when he says his Beloved is like a red, red rose, and we do not think he is infatuated with a plant in his front yard. We know, through the relatively more knowable plant—however mysterious it is as well—enough to know that its image summoned forth is but an analogue to the greater mysterium of the Beloved.

And so we stand before our infinite universe, the ever-unfolding mystery, with its panoply of metaphors: *black holes*, *quarks*, and *ablation* to *albedo* (also an alchemical term) to *Big Bang*, and *Blue Shift*, even to *Blue Moon* ("you found me standing alone..."). Through *Dark Matter* to *Parahelion* and *Photon* (not to be confused with *Phobos*: Fear) to *Red Shift* and *Super Nova Remnant* to *Trojan* to *Virgo Cluster* to *Yellow Dwarf*. What a pandemonia of god-terms, what a mass of metaphora, what an amphitheater of analogs!

In *Symbols of Transformation*, Jung studies the active imagination, or sustained reverie, of an American woman living in Geneva whose real name was Frank Miller. In studying with psychologist Theodore Flournoy, Ms. Miller provides an example of a phantasy narrative that had apparently arisen spontaneously from her inner life and dramatizes her emotional isolation, desire for a hero partner, and yet fear of the serpent of sleep that could dash such consummate hopes. While there are certain allusions to images from her conscious life, she further unfolds a mythopoetic summons of the hero energy to rise out of the lethargic, telluric powers of the unconscious, only for that regressive serpent to bite the heel of her animus-carrier

Chiwantopel, an Aztec chieftain. Jung diagnoses this toxification of the hero energy as a fatal dissociation that threatens her ego stability. Years later, in his 1925 seminars, he further recognizes that he was projecting his own semimorbid anima state onto the text of Ms. Miller's narrative. As he was able to track how Ms. Miller's unconscious autonomously sought those elements that urgently required expression from deep within her, so he was able later to track his own autonomous processes in his midlife passage in a work we now know of as *The Red Book*. In his work first on Ms. Miller and then upon himself, he discovered for all of us the usefulness of finding the particular images behind our emotions and thereby begin that most difficult of conversations: the *Auseinandersetzung*, or dialogical exchange between ego consciousness and the unconscious.

Additionally, Jung defined that energy which produced such images as deriving from "the transcendent function." Jung posits that the self-regulating system we call our psyche seeks its own healing and wholeness; thus image formations that carry transformative energies in bodily states, affective expressions, dream images or symptoms participate in both the conscious and unconscious fields and are apprehensible to both. When consciousness can align its hierarchy of choices with the seeming guidance from the unconscious, the person will experience healing, energy flow, and a general feel of the rightness of one's life at that moment. Most of the time we experience, and override, the promptings from the unconscious, but to be able to ally with them is to serve a developmental, healing agenda. To be able to stand on the bridge traversing these two energy streams, without slipping

is profoundly creative, drawing from the detritus of the past, and borrowing from the not-yet to bring forth new images of the possible.

Of the thousands of dreams with which I have worked as an analyst, just let me summarize two to provide illustrations. In one, a 70-year-old man, about to undertake a rescue mission for his forty-some-year-old daughter in another city, dreams he is with a magician in tuxedo and top hat, which he associated with his analyst. Together they are called upon to perform an autopsy on the dreamer's long dead Mother. As they reluctantly near the casket, the corpse arises to reveal it is instead his deceased wife, who announces that she is back and that "she rules here." She ascends from the casket, kisses the dreamer with a bitter, acidic kiss on the lips and floats away, leaving him shaken.

First of all, who would consciously make up something like this dream? Throughout his life, he had been conditioned to take care of a wounded woman, beginning with his mother, electing to marry a troubled woman who died earlier of chronic alcoholism, and at the time of the dream he is about to embark on another mission of rescue. While one would not, in the abstract, criticize a father offering help to a daughter, the dream arose to tell him that this was one more chapter in a long history of his captivation by a "story." In that story, he had no choice but to associate with, and take care of, the wounded other. Two of the specific personages were now dead, but the narrative they formed was alive and still compelling him.

In this dream, we see the Faulknerian adage that the past is not dead and that it is not even past. The recognition of patterns in our lives, especially those that undermine our own legitimate self-interest, is ample testimony to the living presence of affect-laden, imaginal threads with the power to compel ego assent, provide ready rationalizations to legitimize the complex, and enact the script to which that image is attached. Such images ripple through our lives, steer the course of empires, and constitute the fate of nations as well.

The problem with a complex is that it has no imagination. Given that its "narrative" may have been a profound epiphenomenal misreading of primal events, and that the individual is quite capable of other courses of action, the monothematic character of a complex dictates an imprisoning cycle on Ixion's wheel, condemned to repetition until countered by a still larger imaginal possibility. The gift of dreams, symptoms, encounters with wisdom literature, and other modes of insight and inspiration are specifically counter to the iron wheel of complex and its grim repetition. The magnificence, the imaginal ingenuity of this dream, the emotional charge, impressed both dreamer and analyst with the recognition of, and the power of, both the determinisms of history playing out unto the third generation, and the presence of some larger force field that wishes his healing, and his release from the iron grip of the goddess *Ananke*, the terrible deity of Necessity.

Let one more example suffice for now. The most memorable dream I received while still in training in Zürich many decades ago came from a German woman who had lost both of her parents during and after World War II. She had known only a harsh stepmother in her developing years. At puberty she became severely bulimic and nearly died. Her life was saved during a stay in a clinic in Zürich. But now, in midlife, she lived alone, had a rigid, severely astringent lifestyle, controlled eating and relational behaviors, and made her living as a translator and language tutor. While gifted intellectually, she had not attempted higher education and lived a very modest life in virtually agoraphobic isolation.

One day she brought a dream whose power had shaken her. She is holding a doll, which she also knows in the dream is the simulacrum of her own childhood, when a witch enters the room and steals the doll. She pursues the witch in panic to retrieve this important doll. The witch refuses money but says she will only return the doll/child if the dreamer performs three tasks (as was so common in the *Märchen* of medieval tradition): make love with a fat man; give a lecture at Universitat-Zürich; and return to Germany to have a meal with her still living stepmother. When the dreamer told her dream, she was well aware of the symbolic tasks the witch's agenda asked. To make love with the fat man would be to come to terms with her body, which had always seemed alien to her, to sexuality, and to intimacy in general when that field of energy had always been painful for her. To give the public lecture would be to embrace her fine mind and her intellective gifts. Most challenging of all, to willingly return to the "evil stepmother," and to break bread with her, would be to break the iron grip of her understandable "story" prejudiced by the dark side of Great Mother, the archetype of life, an encounter that had mostly brought her hurt, denigration, and abandonment.

Again, we see the power of the primal imagination to weave a counterimage to the imaginative embroideries only possible to the child. The ego-imaginal limitations, which constrict us in our "readings" of the phenomenal world, are ultimately countered, corrected, compensated by the larger "reading" that can arise from the soul. When we are able to separate the earlier readings from our identification with them, to see them as "readings," not reality, then we can open to the larger realm that wishes to be expressed in the world through us. In other words, each of us has to learn *we are not what happened to us*, attached as we are to our epiphenomenal stories. *We are what wants to enter the world through us.*

The imaginative range of complexes is severely limiting. The powers of conscious life, ideologies, and cultural forces are also limiting. But encounters with the soul, with the reality of the psyche, summon one to a larger life, a larger risk, a larger imagination than the limiting purview of ego consciousness. As Christopher Fry observed, affairs then become soul-sized. In the end, as noted through Rilke in the epigraph, and Plato before him in *The Meno*, such knowledge is the re-membrance of the soul, which has its locus in a realm much larger than consciousness. Pre-Socratic Heraclitus said that *Soul* is a distant island, so large, vast, that it can never really be approached or described. But we will try to find a way, nevertheless.

Chapter Seven
Narcissus's Forlorn Hope:
The Fading Image in a Pool Too Deep

"What seest thou else
In the dark backward and abysm of time?"

Shakespeare, *The Tempest*

"The deep is the unsayable."
Ludwig Wittgenstein, *Philosophical Investigations*

We all know the outlines of the ancient story of Narcissus and from afar have judged the self-absorption of the youth transfixed by his own image in the pool. We who might pause a moment in the restaurant's mirror, straightening the tie, fluffing the hair, freshening the makeup, can afford such largess for are we not all above such self-absorption as sank this ancient soul?

Narcissus was cursed to have been "seen in his flaw," as we, perhaps, are not, and *Nemesis* chose to catch him up on his one-sidedness. Jung's simplest definition of neurosis was the one-sidedness of the personality, a trait for which we are well rewarded today, and often handsomely paid. Catching his image in the pond, he was captivated, possessed. Again, Jung's term for the experience of a complex was *Ergriffenheit*: seizure, or possession. So captivated by his own beauty, Narcissus's libido turned inward, fed on itself, and he lost the vital erotic vector of life. Life is served by the desire for, the encounter with, the dialogue with the other. This self-absorption is a form of hell. As poet Gerard Manley Hopkins put it, to be one's own sweating self is to be irredeemably mired in our stasis without possibility of movement, dynamism, or growth through engagement with the otherness of the other.

Nemesis is not a god, but one of those impersonal forces—like *Dike*, and *Sophrosyne*—that course through the cosmos and to which even the gods seem to bend. To the degree that any of us feels insecure, that insecurity will show up over and over and over in venue after venue. Nemesis is often found amid a harvest of consequences, consequences that flow from our numerous gaps in consciousness. And wherever we are unconscious, the play of possibility is immense. All cultures, for example, amid their carnival of possibilities have an archetypal presence called "the trickster." The trickster is that figure, god, or animal, or humanoid *jongleur* whose purpose seems to be to upset our apple carts, to remind us that we are not gods, that we are not as knowing, not as much in charge, not as omnipotent as we might think we are. So, Nemesis enchants Narcissus, and he falls into the sickness unto death, the *mortificatio*, the stultification of libido that occurs whenever the dialectic is replaced by one-sidedness, ambiguity by certainty, probing inquiry by fundamentalism, democracy by fascism, and so on.

The first "modern" to really explore narcissism was Fyodor Dostoevski in his 1863 *Notes from Underground*. This perverse, countercultural analysis explored both the collective phantasy of meliorism, the doctrine of "progress," and the phantasy of moral improvement toward which the 19th century believed it moved so confidently. On the collective level, the underground man mocks the narcissistic self-congratulation of the first world's exhibition, the Crystal Palace outside London, a hall of glass in which could be seen not only the tools of the new, progressive epoch, but the self-congratulatory genius that procured them. But the underground man imagines that same technology will be used in the century to follow to more efficiently kill more people than ever before. Little could he envision how prescient his observation and that the ruins of the Crystal Palace were later used as a navigational point by the Luftwaffe in its bombing runs over London, nor that that morally untethered technology would build concentration camps and nuclear weapons less than eight decades later.

But even more telling, the underground man turns his lens upon himself and describes his own naked emotions, and uncensored agendas. "Now then, what does a decent man like to talk about most? Himself, of course. So, I'll talk about myself."[14] His honesty is to this day still astounding and justifies the appellation he grants himself: "the antihero."

He celebrates his capacity to make others miserable when he moans loudly from a toothache. He acknowledges that he has no self-worth because, of course, he is a man of superior

---

[14] Fyodor Dostoyevsky, *Notes from Underground*, p. 93.

is found in an afterlife, a place for a possible transformation through embrace by that transcendent Other. Practically, speaking, the linkage to that transcendent Other is so attenuated today that most people have felt the ground shift beneath their feet, occasioning the stirrings of existential Angst, and have inflated this moment, this hour, with an urgency far exceeding the *carpe diem* thread of classical Greece and Rome. If, as more and more suspect, the Other is not there, or looking elsewhere for a century or two, one must scour one's own image through some transient graffito in the shifting sands of the hourglass.[15]

How often we have heard people say, "I want to know myself," or even we have said it ourselves. But do we, really? Could we bear that? Could we bear the possible revelations that we are "human," *menschliche, alle zu menschliche* after all, with all its anfractuosities, its capacities for brutality and compassion, for selfishness and generosity, for aggression and caregiving? Since most of us would like to think of ourselves as improvements on humanity's earlier developmental history, could we bear to be simply the most recent iteration of the whole human project, as Terence suggested: "*Nihil a me humanum alienum puto.*"

The ancients recognized our ambivalence before the vision in the pond. Could we afford to stare at our own darkness directly, or that of another, or that of Divinity? We know what happened to those who looked at Medusa directly, and so Athena's bright shield provided a reflective surface, a

---

[15] American soldiers left the phrase "Kilroy was here" everywhere in the world during World War II. "Kilroy" got around. And did that mean, "Kill the King?"

distancing prism perhaps, through which to refract that primal power. As T. S. Eliot put it, "Humankind cannot bear too much reality." Jung recognized the role of "resistance," the creation of those

> taboo regions which psychology must not touch.
> But no war was ever won on the defensive; one
> must, in order to terminate hostilities, open
> negotiations with the enemy and see
> what his terms really are.[16]

For over two centuries now, philosophers, psychologists, phenomenologists, physicists, and others have been telling us that we cannot know things in themselves: Hume, Kant, Heisenberg, Husserl, and so on. All we can "know" is that we do not know; but we do experience, and we experience through various modalities, categories, and mediatorial vehicles. Poets and prophets have always known this. The poet knows he or she cannot speak of love or grief or anything worthwhile directly, so he or she will find a tangible object, which, because more nearly available to the corporeal senses, lends itself to the task of bridging to the essential but illusive other. Thus "the beloved other" is wholly "other" to the poet, but he says his love is like a flower, and we immediately get his angle on her. Thomas Nashe, describing the terror of the approaching Black Death, writes: "Brightness falls from the air; / Queens have died, young and fair; / Dust hath closed

---

[16] Jung, *The Practice of Psychotherapy*, CW 16., para. 374.

Helen's eye."[17] We get the point. If you think you are exempt from the roving eye of Lord Death, think again. If we miss that point, he repeats the refrain, *"timor mortis conturbat me."*[18] So, even if we do not dimly see ourselves in that dark glass, we are, apparently, seen by an eye from which we cannot hide.

Remember when you, the reader, first stared into a mirror, perhaps as a toddler, amused to see another, a simulacrum, a funny other who moved limbs like you, yet not you, for that person in the mirror moved differently. How to explain that? Was it that an alternative world lay within, on the other side of that silvered surface? Could one step through into another world, just like this, but not, as through a black hole into an alternative universe? And if so, what did it say about the provisonality of this world, this universe, this I?

Narcissus is judged in our emotionally distanced place because he is captured by, possessed by his self-image, but are we not all captives to some extent? Is that not the problem for all of us? Is not the central task of psychotherapy to examine, identify, what stories, what concepts, what self-images have captivated us, led us to our current impasse, our suffering, and to bring them to the surface, challenge them, and perhaps replace them with something larger, more capacious? Freud called the process *Nacherziehung*, or reeducation, given the need to repair, or redeem the original *paideia*, or "education," that instructed us as to who we were and what we were to do with our lives.

---

[17] Thomas Nashe, "A Litany in Time of the Plague."
[18] "The fear of death troubles me."

When we are young, vulnerable, and utterly at the mercy of the world around us, we desperately "read" the world for clues as to who we are, who the other is, what the world is about, how we are to comport ourselves, and so on. The core perceptions assemble over time into a reticulated, anxiety-driven set of autonomous responses to life's challenges. Were there no psychopathology, namely, the revolt of the *Self* (Jung's metaphor for the deep natural wisdom of the whole organism), we would be nothing but a series of reticulated and adaptive mechanisms. The revolt of the Self tells us that there is an Other within, a transcendent Other. As it is transcendent to the ego consciousness, nothing particularly useful or informative can be said about it; thus, a respectful silence is best. As Wittgenstein put it, *"Wovon man nicht sprechen kann, darüber muss man schweigen."*[19]

So, when we look in the mirror of the world, do we see ourselves, or do we not see through the distorting lenses of our complexes, those charged clusters of history, those fractal narratives that we assemble, some conscious, some not? Is not most of our life seeing what our history tells us, what our world told us, or we thought told us a long time ago? Is not much of our history a replication of the self-image we thought reflected to us?

We are social animals. Those deprived of social inter-action, social mirroring, often suffer from an anaclitic depression and a failure to thrive. We learn a great deal about ourselves as we are reflected in the eyes and reactions of

---

[19] "Whereof one cannot speak, thereof one should remain silent." *Tractatus Logicus Philosophicus.*

others. I have a client currently whose mother repeatedly told him that he was the cause for her unhappy life. What was he to do with that? As a child, was he to take his own life, get out of the way? He thought of that, but then he thought of his younger brothers and knew he couldn't leave them unprotected. So, he labored on through the darkness—drove himself through a life of work, overcompensation, and caretaking of others, and only now, in the sixth decade, is beginning to think of his life reflected in a different pool. As he sends his child off to college, he knows he has made her feel welcome, safe, valued, and empowered to live her own journey. The person she sees in the mirror is quite different from the one her father sees every day. And she had no idea that her father sees himself, or has seen himself, as the unworthy, unwanted impediment in his mother's life all these years. As she heads off to a different journey, I have suggested to him that he share with her something of what her father's life has been so that she can begin to see him as he is, not as the perhaps overcompensated great guy he has been, but as a person who is even more worthy of respect and cherishing than she imagines.

Just as the "Self" is a transcendent Other to ego consciousness, so the encounter with the "Other" as God is unknowable. This makes "theology," if one thinks it through carefully, essentially untenable. The transcendent Other is that about which one cannot speak for only silence is respectful of the transcendence of the mystery; anything short of that is a construing by ego-consciousness and a distortion by com- plexes. As one wit put it, one may be pretty sure we have made the gods in our own image when they seem to hate the same people we hate. (And how much history and contemporary politics does that help explain)? Or, as the ancient Xenophanes observed, if horses and lions could draw, the gods they would draw would look like horses and lions. So, respecting the Self as transcendent Other, means the best we ever get at it is a "sense of self."

In the so-called narcissistic personality disorder, the narcissist has essentially lost connection with the corrective ministries of the Self. Thus, he or she is consumed by a default program: namely, *self-inflation as compensation for the disconnect from the Self.* (This program for living was reportedly critiqued by Pearl Bailey, who noted, "Them whats thinks they is, ain't.") Most of us are simply garden variety neurotics, which means we know we have erred, we suffer our disconnections, know we are at fault, and know we have to get back in line with some deeper principle within. This "knowing" represents our attenuated but still living thread to the Self.

Today, though, we have forgotten much wisdom possessed by those who went before us, we also know too much to reconnect. Blake worried about this over two centuries ago and proposed "reorganized innocence," an oxymoron if there ever was one. William Wordsworth and Rilke grasped the sad solitude of certainties lost forever, of moments of "wholeness" never to be regained. (Most of country music thrives on this dialectic of yearning, loss, and more yearning). And what is it we really long for? Robert Frost, in a poem titled "For Once, Then, Something," reports a moment in his reflection on the matter while staring into a well.

Once, when trying with chin against a well-curb,
I discerned, as I thought, beyond the picture,
Through the picture, a something white, uncertain,
Something more of the depths—and then I lost it.
Water came to rebuke the too clear water.
One drop fell from a fern, and lo, a ripple
Shook whatever it was lay there at bottom,
Blurred it, blotted it out. What was that whiteness?
Truth? A pebble of quartz? For once, then, something.

That canny old Vermonter. He is not writing about a well, and we all know it. He is probing in his usual way what there is to probe "beyond the picture, through the picture," the received story, the conventional ego frame, something tangibly white, momentarily visible in the dark depths. Something-there. (*Da-Sein*?) Something from the depths. Visible at last? But no, a drop of water from a branch effaces the surface, and the image crazes in fractured shards. "What was that whiteness? Truth?" Was it that? Was it the promised truth? The Promised One? Or merely a stone shard, another hoax, another distortion through the glass darkly? Frost's perplexity is ours as well.

I imagine that when we stare into our psychic pool, we experience what, ultimately, Narcissus experienced to his dismay. He wasn't just entranced by his beauty; he was stunned by his complexity, his infinite number of selves, his compelling regression into the black hole of the timeless *Unus Mundi*. Like the Quaker on the box of Quaker Puffed Wheat holding a box of Quaker Puffed Wheat holding a box of Quaker Puffed Wheat that so amused, perplexed, and captivated me as a child at the breakfast table, our image in the pool fades in infinite replication, infinite regression, into a carnival House of Mirrors, a receding puzzle box, a *Matryoshka* doll within a doll within a doll, and so on. Narcissus wishes to be seen, and to be seen, wholly. And valued, as he is. And so do we. The religious affirm that only God has that power, that capacity, and perhaps they are right. Perhaps also the Self is that capacious power within each of us that sees and holds us with care as we tumble though an infinite space into the depths of our own fathomless mysteries.

It is a pool of great depth, a pool too deep for human sight to penetrate, but we urgently look and never stop looking.

Chapter Eight
Theogonys and Therapies:
A Jungian Perspective on Evil

"It's true that the gods live,
But up over our heads, up in a different world.
They function endlessly up there, and seem to care little
If we live or die, so much do they avoid us."
                    Friedrich Hölderlin "Bread and Wine"

Some time ago, I met with a 61-year-old woman who is the daughter of a military couple whose substance abuse and contentious, violent marital relationship caused her and her five siblings to live in hell. One of her mother's many visiting lovers raped her when she was 11. She told no one of this trauma until after reaching 40 years old for she knew that she would be doubly violated as their scorn and blame would be visited upon her rather than her assailant. Throughout her childhood, she rose at 5 a.m. every day to rouse, feed, and dress her younger siblings until she left for college. Driven by a steady hum of anxiety, shame, and self-loathing, she promptly found a man to take her away from all that but who would predictably abuse and betray her. Her self-treatment plan also included residing for decades in the underworld of alcoholism, and had she not had children for whom she felt responsible, she would many times have preferred to take her life to end her pain. Today, sober and productive, she remains in terror of relationship, is afraid of risking feeling anything, and is dying of loneliness. That she has been lost in a very dark wood, to borrow Dante's metaphor, for a very long time is obvious and profoundly grievous. Only now, as she faces the last decades of her life, has she sought therapy to possibly fashion a life not defined by darkness.

However horrible the circumstances of her life, the history of abuse, the chronicles of shame and self-degradation, the relentless angst in which she lives her journey, can we say that she has suffered *evil*? If we use that term as therapists, what do we mean? From whence does such ontological conviction emanate? And how are we to work in its presence? Are we to avoid moral categories and simply manage pragmatic costs with pragmatic treatment plans? When in 1988 Karl Menninger asked, "Whatever became of sin," was he right to redeem this concept for our profession, which so often has treated the darkest of human behavior, as deriving from defective genes, hormonal imbalances, interfering complexes, or cultural relativisms? We are rightly cautioned not to impose our own moral categories, prejudices, complexes onto our clients, but are we then sometimes led to collude, however unwittingly, with evil and its perpetuation? In his fine book *Explaining Hitler: The Search for the Origins of His Evil*, Ron Rosenbaum offers a range of perspectives on contributive factors in making modernism's favorite whipping boy. Having done so, he then raises a disturbing challenge to his own project: Were it possible to "understand Hitler," would it make him less culpable, his monstrous misdeeds less evil? (As the old French proverb has it, "*Tout comprendre, tout pardonner.*")

As therapists, we have to face a basic dilemma: Should we avoid such terms as evil and simply be pragmatic? Do we collude with evil and its perpetuation if we use contemporary euphemisms to describe it, such as "disorder?"

In this essay exploring the subject of "Humanity's Dark Side," I liken the "dark side" of humanity to the Jungian concept of the "shadow," which is mostly unconscious. Ignoring this energy field within each of us leads to self-defeating choices. The shadow side, or "dark side," is dark not only because it may be (but is not necessarily) the repository of "evil," but also because it is the hidden side—that is, the side upon which light does not fall. It is dark because it is ignored or not illuminated. We all have a tendency to not want to face what challenges the self-definitions of the ego world. Facing the dark side, casting light on it, brings it out from the shadow and allows it to potentially be integrated into the personality. If we do not do this, we project the shadow onto others, which can lead to hysteria, scapegoating, and violence. Furthermore, when we ignore our shadow side, we diminish ourselves and live timorous, truncated lives. As Jung once noted, a shadow-less person is a superficial person, a person without values, without commitments, a person governed by chameleonlike adaptations that estrange one from the rich textures of the soul.

Comparative Views of Evil

When we begin to examine the problem of evil and the encounter with both "natural" evil—earthquakes, hurricanes, cancer—and "moral" evil—the suffering that we bring to ourselves or others as a result of our choices—we immediately encounter the "*Shadow*" issue of the Western theological traditions. The Eastern traditions typically embraced a polytheistic view, as in Hinduism, where there are multiple divinities, operating in multiple, diverse ways without contradiction, wherein human hope is vested in the possibility of conducting this phase of a cosmic history in such fashion as to relieve some of the burden for the next incarnation. In Buddhism, the problem is centered in the grasping, imperialistic activities of the insecure but inflated ego, which wishes for control, sovereignty, and an exemption from suffering. For the Buddhist, the key may be found in the transformation of ego consciousness from its delusional effort to control to the relief of "letting be," of going with the flow of energies in constant transformation, and in relinquishing an inflated identification with the ego state as the core of our being.[20]

The Western theologies, however, placed all their chips on the theistic square, the one where there is a single deity: omnipotent, omniscient, omnipresent, and possessing moral character (this last quality not infrequently looking rather like ours, by the way). Given these attributes, such a supreme

---

[20] This idea finds its Western expression in the "Serenity Prayer" of Twelve Step groups, or in the German word for "serenity," *Gelassenheit,* which could literally be translated as "the condition of having let be."

being cannot claim to be looking elsewhere, preoccupied, impotent, or indifferent when suffering or injustice occurs. From this troubling nexus rises the shadow aspect of the Western theologies, a discipline called *theodicy*, whose task it is to explore, perhaps reconcile this core contradiction. No matter how much sophistry or strained logic may be required to make it work out, the unitary nature of divinity is to be preserved at all costs. While many of the arguments of theodicy appeal to the intellect, few satisfy the heart. Moreover, this theodicy project haunts Western therapies also, given our frequently unexamined presuppositions that there is a collective expectation for societal behavior, a putative definition of sanity, and a horror of the amoral as evidenced in our slow terminological evolution from "moral insanity," to "character" disorders, to "personality" disorders, and even perhaps in the contemporary use of the euphemism *disorder* rather than *evil*.

Jung's Concept of the Shadow

It does not require a great deal of psychological awareness to perceive that generally these theologies, these *imago Deis*, arise from projections and often tell us more about the psychic state of the theologian than the mysterious Other. Jung even wrote a book on this subject, *Answer to Job*, recommending cultural psychotherapy for such split tribal or collective imagoes as they shunt the dark side of the cosmos off onto a scapegoat figure, a devil or a Satan, rather than an imago that embraces the totality of being. Such repressive splits Jung named *the Shadow*, which may be experienced on both the personal and the collective level. More recently, an extensive series of letters with Father Victor White, an English Dominican, on the subject of evil has been published. In this exchange, Jung contends with the Roman Church's position that God is the *Summum Bonum*, and resides untouched by evil, evil being merely the *privatio boni*, the absence of the good. Jung rather argues for the ontological status of evil and asserts that any theogony that does not include the dark side of the cosmos is simply incomplete.

Most commonly, the Shadow manifests in our personal lives through the *unconscious* as it spills into one's self-defeating choices, one's narcissistic agenda, or even one's unlived life transmitted to one's children, who carry it into subsequent generations. The greatest burden the child must bear, Jung asserted, is the unlived life of the parent. Thus, wherever we are blocked, oppressed, lacking permission, so our children will be similarly blocked, will struggle in an overcompensated way to break free from our heritage, or will unconsciously evolve a "treatment plan," ranging from anaesthetizing the conflict, to distracting oneself from it, or trying to solve it. In any case, they are still carrying the haunted burden of the disowned past. The way in which many of us in the healing professions carry this vast, impossible assignment of "fixing" what is wrong in others is replicated through what Jung called the archetype of "the wounded healer." It is disgraceful that so many of our training procedures neglect this intrapsychic pathologizing feature, which lies deep within the soul of most therapists and drives many to anxiety, stress, substance abuse, and burnout. This unaddressed configuration alone, this engine of vocational identification, represents one of the prime Shadows of our profession.

The Shadow is not synonymous with evil, *per se*. It is a metaphor to embody whatever ego consciousness, personal or collective, prefers to disown. *That within me which makes me uncomfortable about me, that which I prefer to repress, deny, discard, is my Shadow.* Accordingly, the Shadow may also embody some of my best qualities, such as creativity, desire, spontaneity—all movements of affect that at some point in our development proved costly or contradictory to the norms of our family or cultural context.

The Shadow is *projected onto others*. What I wish to disown in myself I will see in you and condemn it. (The mote in my neighbor's eye is so much more evident than the log in my own). Often, what we dislike most about others is how they embody aspects of our own Shadow. On the collective level, Shadow projection is the origin of bigotry, prejudice, sexism, ageism, and every categorical animosity. The more stressed the cultural climate, the more unconscious and fearful the populace, the more we will seek someone to blame, some scapegoat who may carry the weight of our own psychological laziness. Having personally visited Buchenwald, Mauthausen, Dachau, Bergen-Belson, Auschwitz, and Birkenau, and having read this morning's newspaper, I know that the rail tracks of such projections lead to concentration camps, pogroms, and to killing fields scattered around the planet. And, as I live in an angst-ridden, divided country, I see such Shadow projection manifesting as hysteria, scapegoating, and incitements to violence.

One may also *be subsumed by the Shadow*, and revel in it: *Laissez les bons temps rouler* ("let the good times roll") ... get stoned ... enjoy the pure righteousness of anger ... lose your mind ... bask in the sweet seduction of *Schadenfreude*. As the Shadow contains enormous energy, we often draw upon it, and are exhilarated. As Nietzsche once observed, it is amazing how good bad reasons and bad music sound when one is marching off to meet the enemy.

One may *make the Shadow conscious* and be summoned to humility before its leveling of ego presumptions, fantasies, inflations. Usually we come to this accounting the hard way because of the damage we have done to ourselves or others, or we are called to consciousness by the accumulative debris of consequences, which trail behind our separate histories. Even more, the greatest of our Shadow accounts arises from the narrow, diminished, timid lives we lead. We, and many of our clients, live timorous lives, and our own psyche expresses its contrary point of view through the symptomatology of depression, desuetude, drugs of all kinds—including fundamentalisms, distractions, divertive disorders of desire, and the sundry forms of *mauvais foi* ("bad faith") of which Jean-Paul Sartre accused us. As Jung variously said, we all walk in shoes too small for us. Most of all, we suffer from the general aimlessness of our lives. The summons to Shadow accountability always asks us to grow up, to stop blaming our parents or our partners, and to risk wholeness rather than a conditioned "goodness." While the presenting symptoms our clients bring will vary, most of them are suffering less from the evils of this world than from the unlived life that smolders untended within them.

One might argue that these considerations of the Shadow are more philosophical issues than psychological. To that I would reply that yes, these are philosophical matters, and some of the greatest minds of antiquity wrestled with these same matters. I wish that more therapist training programs paid more attention to philosophy for we are, finally, the sum of our "philosophies," whether conscious or not. Every *complex* is an embodied philosophy, rooted in the subject's past, a splinter personality, a somatic manifestation, a mini-script or scenario, and a tendency toward repetition. Many of our traumata have phenomenologically generated "philo-sophies" of self and world, and all of us have a tendency to commit "the fallacy of overgeneralization," namely, what appeared to be true back then gets extrapolated to subsequent futures and creates those noisome patterns that confound our deepest fantasies of freedom of choice. Would that more therapists were trained in the various argumentative fallacies that philosophers have smoked out through the millennia because our clients and their culture are awash in them. Similarly, however irrational the world is, and how quirky and idiosyncratic our sensibilities, we all could use that old tool, reason, to chart a path through the dark woods of our lives from time to time. And thirdly, developing a mature "philosophy of life," one which asks accountability of us, one which acknowledges the reality of attachment and loss, one which summons us to the highest, will serve anyone well on whatever stormy seas our fate launches us.

Additionally, one of the central virtues of working with dreams is that the client's ego is summoned to a dialogue with a different, deeper source within. The dreams are, after all,

visiting friends. So, too, does the woman who was laughed at by her social worker for talking about the "three hearts housed in her body": one pumped blood, one was broken forever because of the death of her son, and one grieved for the rest of the world. I believe she had greater felt humanity than that social worker, and numerous others on staff who protected their unexamined lives, and fragile hold on things, by ridicule, distancing, and gallows humor. To even keep our one heart open in that place is to invite the minions of hell to enter.

All of us suffer from some PTSD, for life is traumatic, existentially overwhelming, flooding us with a magnitude of experiences too large to wholly assimilate. No wonder we have to repair to sleep to allow the psyche to keep processing that material and metabolizing its toxins. When people are deprived of sleep, and dreaming especially, in laboratory settings over time, they will tend to hallucinate, so urgent is it for that material to be processed. While this engagement with trauma is difficult enough on an individual basis, it may be accumulatively iatrogenic for therapists and professional health care providers as we take in these referred toxins over time. One colleague compared it to invisible silica drifting down from the ceiling, slowly filling our bodies and souls until the *pneuma*, the spirit, is laden, saturated, and finally quenched. I recall one of the senior analysts in Zürich who confessed once that when her week was over, she wept for her most troubled patient. And if they were all doing all right, she wept for herself.

As we know, an elemental treatment for PTSD is to tell one's story over and over, in the company of another trusted other, until that material has been metabolized by the soul again. Without diminishing the encounter with evil that some of our clients have suffered, the therapist has to continuously support the idea that what happen *to* us is not *about* us, as such, though it occupies a regnant portion of our experience. Beneath the level of ego consciousness, we all exercise the mechanism of magical thinking, with paranoid tendencies toward embroidering. "I am what happens to me," we conclude as we internalize our world as a statement *to* us *about* us and continue serving that charged "message."

Reinforcing the idea that the traumata arose from the exigencies of life, from the pathology of another person, from the occasional collusion of time and agency, is critical to developing another region of the psyche that not only can challenge the messages implicate in the trauma, but can learn to govern from a larger psychic space. As Jung said of our core complexes and wounds, we may not solve them, but we can outgrow them.

If we look at humanity's dark side, we are obliged in the name of philosophical honesty to consider whether the idea of *dark*, the idea of *evil* itself, is not primarily an "ego" problem, the problem of splitting when the universe itself is not split—it simply is. As a John Steinbeck character put it, "There ain't no good and there ain't no evil; there's just stuff folks do." In other words, whatever we personify when we speak of nature naturing (*natura naturans*) or nature natured (*natura naturata*), such a force does not consider or care about the problem of evil or of light and dark. What agencies people have personified as "the gods" apparently do not either, although there are, of course, religions such as Christianity whereby a compassionate deity is professed to have entered the world in human form to share and possibly redeem suffering. The polytheisms have an easier time with all this because the divine powers are not obliged to be consistent or compassionate, or anything but the divine Other. Classical Buddhism is accordingly more an existential psychology that addresses our core condition: *angst*. The ego then is not tasked with that impossible agenda of sovereignty, which serves as the core, silent assumption of so many modern psychologies and therapeutic methods. Most of our psychological theories and treatment plans invest heavily in the fantasy of ego sovereignty and control through cognitive restructuring and behavioral modification. These fantasies will, to the classical Buddhist, only deepen delusion and set the ego up for further angst as these stratagems ultimately fail.

Similarly, most popular theologies set up the believer, either by infantilizing him or her through guilt and anxiety, or seducing with intimations of happiness, material prosperity, and longevity. When any of these psychological or theological assumptions falters under the burden of reality, the individual is typically left to account for the discrepancy by indicting the gods, or themselves, for their shortcomings. Gautama noticed this tendency two and a half millennia ago when he said that the ego attitude itself was the problem. Is it not interesting that we are still stubbing our toes on this recalcitrant tendency of ego inflation these many centuries later? And that the implicit healing fantasy of most of our methods may compound this dilemma?

It is the nature of *psyche*, an energy system geared toward its own development and preservation, to differentiate into components that may support or impede those agendas. The phenomenology of being itself splits and creates such epiphenomena as ego consciousness and the splintered fragments of diverse drives, complexes, and reticulated personal and cultural scenarios. These search engines are differentiations of psyche, not unlike the leaf, blossom, stalk, and seed of the plant, and conduct their agenda through multiple structures and functions. Yet, this same utilitarian variegation also begets splits, conflicts, suffering, neurosis. In the Edenic myth, for instance, one may eat of *the Tree of Life*, but *the Tree of Knowledge* is forbidden. Living unconsciously in service to instinct is psychic wholeness; serving the divergent agendas of consciousness, however, leads to fragmentation, inner division, and ultimately spills out into violent contention within one's own species. (We, then, alone among animals, become a problem to ourselves). Various fantasies of "homecoming," of "heaven," of "wholeness," of "happiness," "returning to nature," "the simple life," serve this nostalgia for the lost unity of instinctual being. But there is no going back. The saddest lines in the English language are perhaps those of John Milton describing how our mythopoeic ancestors wound their solitary way out of Eden ... forever.

So, in response, we devise the epiphenomenal armamentaria of theology, psychology, and treatment plans to perpetuate the fantasy of return, forgetting Freud's reminder that our much more modest, perhaps achievable, task is to move from the neurotic miseries of life to the normal miseries of life. While we may or may not agree that the problem of evil, of humanity's "dark side," is the unavoidable casualty of splitting ego consciousness, we will nonetheless have to contend always with the heart and with the irreducible sum of human suffering. As Pascal noted in the 17th century, the heart has reasons that reason knows not. And as Yeats agreed, whatever our theoretic preferences, in the end we are left only "with our blind stupefied hearts."

Bringing The Shadow Into Consciousness

The problem with the unconscious is that it is *unconscious.* We cannot with any certainty say that it exists, yet we have as much right to speak of it as an entity as astrophysicists have to speak of "black holes" whose existence they posit because of their effect on surrounding bodies. That so much of our histories appears to spill into the world from places unknown to consciousness seems to legitimize the existence of such a premise. From the limited purview of consciousness, however, the whole presumption is revolutionary and unsettling. It is unsettling to think that the ego may be only a thin wafer on a large, tenebrous sea when we bank so much on its seaworthy character, ride its tossing structure, and cling to it as a fixity. From the standpoint of the immature, or threatened, ego, even the rest of our psychic reality may be considered a "dark side." The partner of one of my analysands has resisted personal therapy on the grounds that "I know what I think," which is the equivalent of saying, "I think I think what I think." Similarly, the secret imperialism of Freud's "where Id was, there ego shall be" also suggests something of the ego's attitude to this terra incognita. So, in exploring the Shadow, we are asked to be accountable not only for the unknown, but for the little pieces we can know but prefer not to.

In speaking to groups on the theme of the Shadow, I have developed daylong workshops in which, after a general introduction to the concept of the Shadow and examples on the societal and historical front, we explore the theme on a very personal basis. While the privacy of each participant is protected, each is asked to journal on the spot in response to some provocative questions. These workshops have led to some engaging conversations and, I believe, no little increase in personal awareness. While the questions themselves are simple enough, they do stir the pot and bring much otherwise neglected material to the surface. Rather than focus on the issue of evil *per se*, and in the spirit of broadening the topic of humanity's dark side, let me share some of the questions and brief amplifications here.

1. a) *Of your many, many virtues, a list too large to encompass in this brief few hours, can you identify perhaps three of them which you believe show up in your life with reasonable consistency?*

   b) *What are the opposites of those virtues, those manifestations of a darker side to a personality, which of course are most remote from your intentions?*

   c) *Can you identify specific occasions where the practice of the virtues you listed in 1. a) above brought harm to you or someone else?*

   d) *Can you identify specific occasions where the opposite of your virtues, as listed in 1. b) above turned up in your life?*

This very simple, four-part question, begins to shift the ground beneath the ego and its pretensions. All of us wish to think of ourselves as generally righteous people, citizens of good will, and hopefully with beneficent contributions. However, a sober assessment of history, ours and that of the world, suggests that even the very best of intentions may lead to unforeseen harm to self and others. And, however vigilant we wish to be, the whole range of human possibility, sooner or later leaks into the world *through* us. The general effect of these four questions is disquietude and an aroused sensitivity that other forces may be afoot. If anyone ever doubted it, the first question alone begins to underline the role of the unconscious in the governance of daily life and the reminder that we do not, in fact, know what we think, nor are we arrogantly able to chart a course of moral certainty.

2. *Examine the key relationships of your life, domestic and business. Where does the Shadow manifest in patterns of avoidance of conflict or compliance with the pressure of the moment, leading to consequences which are not in your interest or perhaps that of others?*

Again, this question demonstrates the ubiquity of subterranean agendas, old patterns of adaptation, Quisling-like evasions of accountability that allow us to slip-slide away from the encounter with the anfractuosities of life.

3. *Examine the patterns of your intimate relationships, either current or past. What annoys you most about that partner? Where have you encountered such annoyance before?*

This question begins to get at the question of how we project our Shadow onto our partners, and indeed even may select them in order to do so. We chose them for good reasons, and only a very few of those reasons were conscious. In the face of highly charged messages, especially those unconscious, we have a tendency to serve the instructions through repetition, or we may be caught in overcompensation by trying to get away from a dynamic pattern (and thereby being still defined by it), or by having worked out a treatment plan such as a numbing addiction, a life of distraction, or—gasp—being a therapist and trying to fix them in everyone else.

4. *Where do you repeatedly undermine your interests, shoot yourself in the foot, cause yourself familiar griefs? Where do you avoid risking what you intuit to be your larger self?*

Again, the Shadow manifests most tellingly in our collusion with it. Even when we know what is needed, we often repeat patterns compulsively. As Paul said in the *Letter to the Romans*, though we know the good, we do not do it. Why? He tended to mark it up to "sin," the impossibility of perfection, and a dilatory will. All of that may be true, but he did not know much about the vastness of the unconscious and the fact that the contrary tendencies are also part of who we are. In fact, the most astute psychological comment ever to come from the ancient world is from the Roman playwright Terence, who two millennia ago said, "*Nothing* human is alien to me." This self-evident truth is the essence of Shadow recognition, our common humanity, and yet each of us will have some place in our life where denial, evasion, suppression, repression, projection, or dissociation is reflexively employed to distance us and preserve the ego's fragile frame. None of us will wish to access our inner sociopath, embrace the murderer within—though we murder something vital within us on a daily basis—confess our rampant narcissism, and none of us will want to admit how much we want to love and be loved.

5. *Where are you "stuck" in your life, blocked in your development? What fears stand as sentinels to keep you from where you want to go, and from whence do they derive?*

I have asked this question now on four continents, and no one, no one, has ever asked me, "What do you mean *stuck*?" They ask for examples of every other question, but for this one they all start writing in a matter of seconds. It is of considerable psychological import that we can so readily identify where we are stuck, and yet stay stuck. Often the pushback from those stuck places is reinforced by repeated failed attempts to get unstuck, and the person is further afflicted with shame, guilt, and diminished self-esteem. In addressing this question, I acquaint them with the chief premise of depth psychology, namely, that *it is not about what it is about*. Whatever the "stuck" place is, it is not about that issue, for that issue or task is on its own easily addressed. Rather, a metaphoric filament reaches down from the stuck place to a primal, archaic zone of the psyche where the earliest lessons about the twin threats to our survival—over-whelmment and abandonment—were first met and suffered. In these superficial "stuck places," we repeatedly activate primal, archaic anxieties, and it is the admixture, the fuelant from this archaic realm that overpowers the repeated efforts of ordinary ego consciousness to move forward. When one has grasped that "it is not about what it is about," then one can begin to realize that the archaic parts of the blocking mechanism can be confronted by the powers and resiliency the person has acquired over the intervening years. So many persons, whether it presents as writer's block, the need to lose weight, address an addiction, whatever, expressed a relief and a new resolve when they realized that the blockage arose not from their shaky will but from matters long ago and far away, matters that an enlarged consciousness can now address.

6. *Where do mother and father still govern your life, either through repetition, overcompensation, or your special "treatment plan"?*

The unlived life of parents, wherever they were stuck, becomes for all of us a compelling model, script, set of marching orders, or we spend enormous energy trying not to repeat our mother's life, or be like our father, or we evolve sophistic strategies to massage this issue and ignore its continuing role in our lives.

7. *Where do you refuse to grow up, wait for clarity of vision before risking, hope for external solutions, expect rescue from someone, or wait for someone else to tell you what your life is about?*

This question, like the one on "stuckness" is one to which the participants quickly respond. They, we, all know where we are avoiding showing up in our lives. All of us are aware where we would like someone else to take care of this nettlesome journey for us. All of us want to figure it all out, have the ambiguities resolved before we step into the abyss. This deferred accountability, this disowned personal authority, this evasion of responsibility is common to each of us in some area of our lives and is one of the chief manifestations of humanity's dark side. For those of us committed to democratic values, this flight from personal accountability not only sabotages the depth and integrity of our personal journey, but undermines the maturation necessary for a responsible, participatory democracy. No wonder our public sensibilities are characterized by their susceptibility to demagogues and gurus, seduction by fads and fashions, exhibit a short attention span, manifest a ready tendency to scapegoat, prefer simplistic solutions to complex matters, and relinquish personal authority so easily in times of distress. As one of Bertolt Brecht's characters said in response to how a fascist tyranny is created: One doesn't have to organize the criminals, one has only to organize the people. As a result, the darkest side of our collective social structures has its origin in what we have avoided in our personal development. And, as Jung observed of Hitler, in a disordered time, the people chose the most disordered among them to lead them. So have other nations, much more recently.

Meaning Arises From Suffering

In standing on this spinning planet, and doing this kind of work on a daily basis, we cannot help but be thrown back on existential perplexities: Why is there so much suffering, so much injustice? To what degree does one adopt a neutral, uninvolved approach? When is intervention possible, and necessary? How does our own philosophical Weltanschauung help or hinder our work? Is there a legitimate connection between theogony and therapy, and if so, what?

A long time ago, the problem of evil, injustice, the ubiquity of suffering sent me to study philosophy and theology at the graduate level. As rich and provocative as those texts proved to be, I came to appreciate philosopher A. N. Whitehead's critique of "the bloodless dance of categories" and was left with little more than my own blind and stupefied heart (to use a phrase from Yeats). I recall listening to an interview over my car radio on November 23, 1963, as Kenny O'Donnell reflected on the assassination of his kinsman the day before. He said, "What's the good of being Irish if you don't know that sooner or later the world is going to break your heart." One does not have to be Irish to find our personal appointment with the darkest hour. Since that time, I have come to the conclusion that most of us no doubt reach, or we burn out, or we have to close up our spiritual shop and become automatons, namely: The ubiquity of suffering and injustice is pretty much a steady state. Just because we have been distracted for the moment does not remove the fact that horrible things are happening to people in any given moment. All we can bring to the table, then, is compassion, a steadiness that can sometimes assist healing, and the interpretive skills to help people find their position relative to their suffering. In his marvelous updating of the Job story, Archibald MacLeish moves his central character, a businessman named J. B., to observe that God does not love; God simply is. "But we do," his wife, Sarah, reminds him.

Sometimes we can help reframe the patient's suffering without evading it in any way. In the book *Swamplands of the Soul*, I make the point that in every swampland visitation— depression, loss, betrayal, guilt, *et al.*— there is always a psychological task, the addressing of which may move a person from victimage and diminishment to proactive engagement and psychospiritual enlargement. Mysteriously, healing often arises out of the therapeutic alliance itself, this most intimate of relationships. Well over a century ago, Pierre Janet observed what he called "the talking cure," the peculiar phenomenon that people somehow felt better having simply shared their suffering with him. What we can discern in this phenomenon is the importance of human relationship, of one person bearing witness to the suffering of another, and of being held in one's fallen state without judgment.

Surely, one of the most delusory of ideologies in our cultural context is the fantasy of *happiness*. Happiness is a most transient state, and always contextual. (Remember the banquet of Damocles and his sword swinging over the head of the engorged diner?) When we are doing what is right for our soul, that is, *psyche*, we will be flooded from time to time by happiness, but the steady pursuit of it will lead to addictive behaviors, trivialization, and increased suffering. On the other hand, if the goal is *meaning*, that is, finding our purpose in our particular corner of the dark wood, then we will feel the richness of our journey. Part of our therapeutic task, so often necessary, is to undertake Freud's idea of *Nacherziehung*, namely, the reeducation of our values. Helping a person find his or her task amid suffering, loss, disappointment, moves him or her toward greater autonomy.

Analytic psychology, as articulated by Jung, is ultimately a therapy of meaning. Although we begin our work in such swamplands as psychopathology, we are more importantly directed toward the task of finding meaning in those dismal places. What, in the face of these circumstances, is one called to *do*? What new attitudes are required, what persistence of will, and what changing agenda of values does this moment ask of one's life? When these questions are addressed directly, the person stays less stuck on the wounding and more engaged in the task that can lead him or her to enlargement. In the end, the attainment of happiness can be a trivial definition of life, but a more concerted dialectic among heart, brain, and soul may lead to a life well lived, a life in which one finds dignity, autonomy, and worth.

Jung repeatedly observed that we cannot take clients further than we have gone ourselves. Where we are stuck, the therapy will get stuck. We therefore have to bring to the table our own ongoing reflection, our own awareness of blind spots, and our own willingness to acknowledge what we do not know. We will not finally understand humanity's dark side, but we are here to bear witness, to bring the gift of compassion and shared journey to the client. All of us are in the same dark woods, albeit with different paths opening for us. Over eight centuries ago, the writer of the Grail legend noted that when each knight took off in search of the Grail, each one went to a place in the forest where there was no path, for it would be a shameful thing to take the path someone has trod before. Before we can accompany people on their journey through their dark wood, we have to have undertaken our own. Wherever our own courage and resolve to see it through flags or fails, we will fail our patient, for what we have most to share with them is not our learning or our techniques, but rather who we have become and what darkness we have faced in the world and in ourselves.

Chapter Nine

The Rag and Bone Shop of the Heart:
Yeats's Path from Puer Aeternus to Wise Old Man

"Do the people in the orange jumpsuits individuate, and if so, how"? According to the student lore at the Jung Institute in Zürich, this question was likely to come up in an exam, though I never heard of anyone who had actually been asked that question. The point behind this rather Zenlike query was to oblige the trainee to define *individuation*, whatever that is, and to be able to differentiate that individuation did not in any way depend on intelligence, station in life, or even consciousness. The people in the orange jumpsuits were the street cleaners—the ubiquitous presences in the salubrious streets of Zürich, where I often saw them scrubbing streets, public buildings, and trams in the midst of downpours.

So, what, then, was, is, *individuation*? Briefly put, it is incarnating the fullest possibility one can become, being less at odds with oneself, fulfilling the intent of nature, or the gods, a process far more likely achieved through natural unfolding than conscious intent or a conceptual grasp of Jungian principles. Thus, the folks in the orange jumpsuits living closer to nature likely had a much better chance at it than the splendid neurotics we were as trainees.

The individuation process is an unfolding in service to a numinosity, a *telos*, an implicate destiny, a movement of soul toward something indefinable yet compelling. When on track with this possibility, we are not spared suffering, nor do we win the plaudits of our tribe, but we may feel an inner confirmation, perhaps a sense of a supportive energy. When we do not feel these accords, some of us are driven to that examination of, and dialogue with, the soul that is contained in the etymology of the word *psychotherapy*.

****

This essay illustrates aspects of an individuation process as exemplified in the life and work of one person, William Butler Yeats (1865-1939), whose productive life spanned the late romantic, Victorian, and high modernist periods of Western culture. He won the Nobel Prize in 1925, not for his poetry, but for his revival of the Irish theater and for his contributions to the preservation, even resurrection, of a fading Celtic language and culture. When I was a callow youth in my 20s, I chose Yeats for my doctoral dissertation. I believed at the time it was because his poetry was memorable and resonant for me, though I could not explain why. Intuitively, I chose the theme "patterns of opposition and reconciliation in the life and work of Yeats," a very Jungian leitmotif. (One chapter of that dissertation, the sole copy of which I have long since misplaced, was a "Jungian" interpretation of his work, in addition to literary, biographical, theological, and symbolic chapter foci to satisfy the expectations of a diverse committee.) In retrospect, I think I chose Yeats because something in my soul intuited that his journey, which he described as articulately as anyone could, foretold my own daunting agenda. He had traveled that path and left articulate mentoring tracks for me and others.

In the course of research, I learned that there is an incredible overlap between his concepts, his psychology and symbology, and Jung's, a convergence that I described in an early article published and reprinted by *Psychological Perspectives.* Jung had once consulted a translation of the *Upanishads,* which Yeats had edited, and Yeats referred very tangentially to Jung, but they had no direct or sustained contact or even mutual influence. What they had in common was a rejection of the reductive materialist features of modernism, an appreciation for the symbolic life, and a special interest in occult studies as a path to Gnostic wisdom, that is, direct, personal experience rather than received authority. Thus, as intuitives, they mined the same depths, whether as psychologist or as artist. No wonder their insights so often coincided.

Through the years I have drawn upon Yeats at different times in my personal journey as I arrived at junctures similar to which he had earlier traversed. While many casual acquaintances of Yeats will cite a line or a poem from one stage of his life or another, the serious student of Yeats will recognize that there was no single Yeats. There are many Yeatses. He periodically reinvented himself and launched a whole new style, new subject matter, new psychology, new aesthetics. On one occasion, criticized for his changes, and leaving his audience behind, he replied,

> My friends have it I do wrong
> Whenever I remake my song.
> They should know what issue is at stake:
> it is myself that I remake.

This remaking of his identity is how Yeats's individuation organically unfolded. Articulate as he was, and remains, we can track that developmental process through his writing.

* * * *

Yeats was born to a minority Protestant family the last year of the American Civil War, the year Lincoln died, into a largely Catholic culture, an occupied nation, and a country in great danger of losing its soul. How can one sustain one's connection to one's tribal history, one's connective mythos, when the use of one's language is forbidden, when one groans in poverty, when the laws of the occupiers are exploitative, and when one's martyrs are fading memories in the onslaught of a seductive materialism? (His countryman Joyce described Ireland as "an old sow that eats her farrow.") For Yeats, the aristocracy who supported the arts and transmitted cultural values, and the peasants who tilled the soil and sustained the rich mythographic world through story and belief, were being replaced by a nation of shopkeepers, of petit bourgeoisie, who "fumble in the greasy till" and "add half pence to the pence." His personal journey of psychological development would necessarily have to play out in the context of a social, religious, political and aesthetic *Zeitgeist* he considered vulgar, diminishing, and antithetical to his soul and the soul of ancient Eire.

His father, John Butler Yeats, was the premier portrait painter of his era, a flamboyant nonconformist, a man whom Yeats found impossible to rebel against because his old man had already led the rebellion. This artistic spirit and iconoclastic talent spread through the family, for William's brother Jack succeeded his father as probably the most important painter in modern Ireland, and his sisters Lilly and Lolly founded the Cuala Press, which produced lovely, artistically rendered volumes of verse that remain collector's items to this day. (Only the Wyeth family, with its generations of succeeding talent, offers an analogy to the Yeats tribe). In this context, William betook himself to an art institute for a few semesters but found that his talent was in a different medium. This brief education constituted his only formal learning, although he was widely if eccentrically reading all his life.

As flamboyant as his father was, Yeats's mother, Susan, was quiet, reserved, spiritual, and wholly lacking in aesthetic interest. "Sensitive and deep-feeling but undemonstrative, she always considered her birthplace, the romantic county of Sligo, the most beautiful place in the world, and she passed on the feeling to her children ... she stood for a different kind of life, where an ignorant peasant had more worth than a knowledgeable artist." Between these poles of extravertive artist and political rhetorician, and an introvertive, myth-ridden, dreamer, W. B. Yeats lived his life. Theirs was a life of genteel poverty in Dublin and London. Just after they arrived in London, his mother had a stroke, which deprived her of her faculties and invalided her the last 14 years of her life.

Yeats's earliest poetry, from 1885-1903, is characterized by nostalgia for a simpler life, by ambivalence toward the harsh demands of daily reality, a rejection of materialism as a value, and a general tentativeness toward virtually everything conflictual. His is the psychology of the eternal youth, the *puer*, who is bound still to the Mother, not necessarily the personal Mother, but to an overweening desire for security, satiety, and satisfaction: "O sick children of the world … words alone are certain good." ("The Song of the Happy Shepherd") "Come away, O human child / For the world's more full of weeping than you can understand." ("The Stolen Child")

In that same period, he affiliates with the Irish Republican Brotherhood, which morphs into the later IRA, joins occult groups such as The Order of the Golden Dawn, and meets the love of his life, Maud Gonne, a fiery revolutionary. He believes that her commitment to political solution and his to cultural resurgence might, together, provide a healing energy to their stricken nation. He proposes marriage to Maud several times over the next decades, but she repudiates his lifestyle by marrying a soldier of fortune, and abuser, named John McBride. Yeats never gets over this wound. He pines, he complains, he idolizes the Beloved by exalting her in his verse to the status of Helen of Troy and presciently wonders if her political incitements will lead to still another burning city as it does in the Easter Rising of 1916. At times, he approaches the pathetic. In "He Wishes for the Cloths of Heaven," he laments that he can only offer the beloved his plaintive entreaties, for

… I, being poor, have only my dreams;
I have spread my dreams under your feet;
Tread softly because you tread on my dreams.

Finally, he is pulled out of the dreamy world of romance by being sexually initiated by a married woman, Olivia

Shakespear, whose daughter later marries Ezra Pound. The first hint of concrete sexuality and of engagement in the concrete world appears: "The horses of Disaster plunge in the heavy clay: / Beloved, let your eyes half close, and your heart beat / Over my heart, and your hair fall over my breast." ("He Bids His Beloved Be at Peace")

By 1903, Yeats is much changed. Maud has married his rival and moved on. He has found other lovers. He has co-founded The Abby Theatre with Lady Gregory and launches the revival of an independent Irish theater, drawing heavily upon Celtic mythology and peasant lore for its subject matter. The daily demands of running a theater, engaging in political and cultural clashes that their plays provoke, and suffering Maud's rejection matures him and his verse hardens in diction. Like other *puers*, he is called to the differentiation and grounding of his libido, to learn his craft, and to get a job.

When he reaches midlife, he acknowledges the cost of being a high flyer. In his poem "Pardon Old Fathers," he begs,

Pardon that for a barren passion's sake,
Although I have come close on forty-nine,
I have no child, I have nothing but a book,
Nothing but that to prove your blood and mine.

* * * *

So, how do we change? Do we change at all? Do we stay pretty much the same throughout? The answer surely is yes to all of the above. Sometimes we change because our nature is naturing; and sometimes we succumb to an insurgency from below, throbbing and pushing us into life. Sometimes we change because we are carried by the rites, the instructions, the institutions of our culture. Sometimes trauma changes us, if it does not stick us, fixate our growth. Yeats changed from all of the above, and something else, a growing consciousness that brought him *intentionality*, the intentionality to find his own authority, to risk rejection, and to stand for something, even if he were standing alone. At midlife, asking himself what he has brought to the table of life, he writes "A Coat."

I made my song a coat
Covered with embroideries
Out of old mythologies
From heel to throat;
But the fools caught it,
Wore it in the world's eyes
As though they had wrought it.
Song, let them take it,
For there's more enterprise
In walking naked.

For a person who so carefully cultivated the aesthetic, who reveled in "song" for song's sake, his boldness is a step out into an unprotected place. He has cast off the dreamy Celtic twilight (what Joyce cynically called "the cultic twalet") for a more direct presence in this world.

1916 brings the world crashing back down upon him and upon Ireland. The Easter Revolution erupts. Dissidents occupy the General Post Office in Dublin and, after a few heroic, confusing days, are shelled into submission by English gunboats diverted from the Great War. But the British badly stumble in the court of public opinion by ceremoniously executing the 16 rebel leaders, among them Yeats's nemesis, John McBride. That, followed by an occupation by the hated constabulary troops, known as the Black and Tans for their motley uniforms, creates a groundswell of resistance for six years, leading in 1922 to the partition of Ireland into the two regions we know today. Out of this catastrophe Yeats writes the magnificent "Easter, 1916," in which he oxymoronically sees in the crimson effusion of blood the reinvigoration of Irish green, whereby "a terrible beauty is born."

Shortly after the death of McBride, Yeats proposes marriage again to Maud Gonne, who once again demurs, whereby he foolishly proposes to their daughter, Iseult, who has the good sense to decline as well. So much for idealized projections.

In 1917, Yeats finally marries Georgiana, a much younger Englishwoman whom he met in an occult society, and they construct a reasonably happy marriage with two children. On the fourth day of their marriage, Georgiana, seeing that Yeats is still pining for Maud, begins automatic writing (a form of "active imagination"), which purportedly contacts the spirit world and brings enormous revelations. Yeats is so excited that he offers to give up his literary career to be the secretary of these immanent powers, but fortunately for modern literature, they reply that they have rather come to provide him metaphors for his poetry. From that point on, many of Yeats's poems can be read at two levels, a surface available to the casual reader and a Gnostic level, which alludes to a whole cosmology, a theory of personality types, and an interpretation of history that he published in 1927 as *A Vision* and revised and republished in 1934. The well-known poem, "The Second Coming," is but one of these twin-tiered structures.

For his many articulations of political vision, Yeats is appointed a senator in the first Irish parliament. He serves conscientiously for two terms from 1922-28. But what most characterizes the last two decades of his life is that familiar Jungian theme—the tension of opposites. So many of his poems are dialectic structures in which he argues the opposites within his own nature. As he writes in "Ego Dominus Tuus,"

> By the help of an image
> I call to my own opposite, summon all
> That I have handled least, least looked upon.

Jung spoke of the work of analysis as an *Auseinandersetzung*, the setting of one thing over against another. Throughout the life and work of Yeats one finds this recurrent dialectic.

Surely, the most important conversation we ever have is with ourselves over the polysemous meaning of our unfolding journey. Out of the quality of this conversation, the quality of all other conversations with others necessarily follows. In his "Dialogue of Self and Soul," Yeats's conversation culminates in a profound affirmation. Surveying his tortuous, tumultuous life, he concludes, "I am content to live it all again." How many of us can reach the end of our journeys and affirm all that has been, *all* that has been?

No young person is granted leave to write those concluding words. When Yeats wrote them, he was ailing in body and suffering in spirit, yet full of that towering affirmation that signals an elision from the *puer*, afraid of the world, to the wise old man who has entered it, suffered in body and spirit there, and come through.

> When such as I cast out remorse
> So great a sweetness flows into the breast
> We must laugh and we must sing,
> We are blest by everything,
> Everything we look upon is blest.

In the 1930s, Yeats declines in body but not in soul. On his deathbed, he writes still of Maud Gonne, the great unrequited love of his life, and two poems of the many he included in *Last Poems* (1936-39) stand out for honoring the great dialectic of his journey, and ours: a loving commitment to this world and an affirming release from it. (As Frost said of himself, Yeats also had a lover's quarrel with the world).

In "Lapis Lazuli," he considers the social disorders of his time, anticipates another world conflagration (which commences, in fact, the year he dies) and achieves a Buddhistic "releasement" from the 10,000 passing things of this world. His adumbration that "aeroplane and Zeppelin will come out" proves prescient in the imminent Luftwaffe assaults, even as these alarms and discords transmogrify an old, old story for "there struts Hamlet, there is Lear. / That's Ophelia, that Cordelia" who "do not break up their lines to weep. / They know that Hamlet and Lear are gay." Above and beyond history, an archetypal drama plays out, for above the troubled plain, the sages sit and "on all the tragic scene they stare," but, and it is a profound *but*, after years of public opposition, political hurley-burley, vituperation, jealousy, and defeat, he is able to affirm this tension of opposites, and let go:

> Their eyes mid many wrinkles, their eyes,
> Their ancient, glittering eyes are gay.

Again, only oxymoron, only the paradox of "tragic gaiety," is large enough to embrace the very opposites the *puer* sought to avoid through his aesthetic flight. Only "tragic gaiety" embraces wisdom by transcending polarities through the paradox of acceptance/release, and relinquishment/affirmation.

In this same period, late fall of 1938, Yeats rises from his bed, asks of Maud, and writes his political and aesthetic will, "Irish poets, learn your trade, / Sing whatever is well made," and consigns himself to the dust beneath his beloved County Sligo mountain Ben Bulben:

> Under bare Ben Bulben's head
> In Drumcliff churchyard Yeats is laid.
> An ancestor was rector there
> Long years ago, a church stands near,
> By the road an ancient cross.
> No marble, no conventional phrase;
> On limestone quarried near the spot
> By his command these words are cut:
> *Cast a cold eye*
> *On life, on death.*
> *Horseman, pass by!*

So, is this is the final word from this passionate man, this breezy detachment from what he once called "the fury and mire of human veins"? Perhaps.

Yeats died in Roquebrunne, France, in January of 1939 and was buried in a communal grave. The outbreak of the Second World War that same year meant that the world turned to other things until 1948, when the Irish government sent the corvette *Macha* to the Riviera to bring his remains home in state. When his body was piped off the ship in Galway harbor, filled still today with the swans he loved for their archetypal beauty and hint of longevity, his body was received by the Irish minister of the interior, one Sean Gonne McBride, the son he never had with Maud. (Subsequent research has indicated that Yeats's remains were identified from the communal grave by the fact that he was wearing a metal truss for a hernia condition. At the same time, an Englishman was buried in the same grave as Yeats, also with a metal truss, so that today it is a 50-50 chance that Yeats's grave in Drumcliff Churchyard is occupied by that Englishman, one Alfred N. Hollis. (As a wag in Houston once said, "Who's buried in Yeats's grave? Could be Hollis").

Yet, I think that the same Yeats who, during the last years of his life, described himself as a wild, wicked, passionate old man, the one who wrote a series of bawdy ballads spoken by a "Crazy Jane" persona, is more to be found among his last poems in "The Circus Animal's Desertion." In this poem, Yeats reviews his life and compares himself to a ringmaster at a circus, one who summoned many personae in his tour, many stunning animalia, many high-wire balancing acts, and now knows that the show is closing. The aesthetic sleight of hand which once offered the *puer* the means of escape, what he terms the "ladder" up and out of the muck and mire, has disappeared. But then he considers from whence those early images of flight, those midlife images of conflict, and those late-life images of acceptance and transcendence emerged. Yes, all those images once

> Grew in pure mind, but out of what began?
> A mound of refuse or the sweepings of the street,
> Old kettles, old bottles, and a broken can,
> Old iron, old bones, old rags, that raving slut
> Who keeps the till. Now that my ladder's gone,
> I must lie down where all ladders start,
> In the foul rag-and-bone shop of the heart.

Does this sound like the youth who sought refuge in the imaginary, or escape through the transports of aesthetic sleight of hand? The raving slut who tends the till for all of us is time, death, and desiccation, and she returns us all to elemental earth. But encased in this rag/flesh and bone/cage the heart beats on. We are left with our humanity, our yearning for love, for divinity, for release, yet are returned finally to the heart that, thumping its disquietude still, opens to life, to death, and to the great mystery of it all.

Yeats moved from the eternal youth to the wise old man. He earned his way. We who follow must beware of seeking wisdom, lest we have to earn it too. We are grateful for the markers he left behind in the dark wood we all enter, but each of us must find our personal path through, as he did his.

Chapter Ten
The Necessity of Personal Myth

"Untune that string, and hark what discord Follows."
                    Shakespeare, *Troilus and Cressida*

"The world is full of people whose notion of a satisfactory
future is, in fact a return to an idealized past."
                    Robertson Davies

What is *myth*, and why is it necessary to have a personal
myth? *Myth*, as I am using the word here, represents *the
energy-charged values to which we are in service, whether
consciously or not, and the goals they serve, whether consciously
or not.* Our myths drive us, make our choices, and only a
portion of their presence is ever brought to the surface of
consciousness. Did you ever look back and ask yourself, "Why
did I do that?" "Why did I make such wrong choices, such
counterproductive investments in my life?" Who has not had
such moments of chagrin upon moments of reflection?

What we do in our lives, as we have noted elsewhere in
this book, comes from many sources: our DNA, our ancestral
voices, our charged clusters of history known as *complexes*.

Neurological studies have indicated that we, priding ourselves on our exalted levels of awareness, actually are driven 95% of the time by the unconscious. In fact, studies in the 1980s have demonstrated that decisions are made in the unconscious before consciousness even knows it has a decision to make. As that car hurtles toward you, your psyche has begun to react milliseconds before you see, say "danger" to yourself and step back. So much for our pious belief in our sovereign consciousness.

In most cultures before the recent centuries, individual life was pretty much governed by the structures, cultic practices, and values of the tribe, mediated through the teachings of the elders, the sages, the prophets. Moreover, the "stories" belonging to the tribe, those given by "the gods" to their ancestors, mediated the individual with the mysteries and the terrors of a recondite nature. Those stories, charged with energy sufficient to move a person's soul helped link to the four orders of mystery in which all humans live their journey, up through the present time, namely:

The Cosmos: Is this an ordered universe, as the word *cosmos* suggests, or a random concatenation of events that inexplicably affect us and for which we have the word *chaos*? This question is very much with us today, even we are now able to see ordering patterns in chaos itself. If there is an order, who or what are the Orderers? Are they "the gods." Why are we here? What is their will for us? Wither do we go after this life?

The Environment: Where do we fit in the natural world? What happens when we run afoul of nature, when nature turns on us, as so many of us have seen increasingly happen.

We have clearly lost a relationship to the natural world and the mutual respect that includes a future. Global warming, the disappearance of thousands of species, the pollution of the air, sea, and land is beginning to build an autonomous counterreaction that will literally imperil human life on this planet in this century. Perhaps our recent pandemic, as well as disastrous hurricanes and forest fires, is nature's retort to our depredation. Perhaps fewer of us will do less damage to our home.

The Society: What is my social identity? Who am I, as defined by tribe, geography, social categories? Do I even have a tribe, a sense of belonging to something? What are the rights, duties, and obligations of being a social being? What are the legitimate claims of "the social contract," as Rousseau described it?

The Journey of the Self: What are the points of reference that help me make my choices? What allows me to differentiate the plethora of values bombarding me and find and live my own? What, specifically, is my journey, separate from the trajectories of so many others?

****

These life questions obviously persist and are compelling whether we bring them to the surface of consciousness or not. If we don't, we can be sure we are living received values, not ours, and they may or may not prove healthy for us, or supportive of our journey.

Just as affect-laden images move and shape individuals, so they form cultures, and generate their systems, values, and marching orders. As long as that culture's images speak to the hearts and minds of its members, the myth is living, charged, and links one to transcendent values. When, however, any cultural form begins to lose that energy, no longer moves the heart, it devolves into a concept, a dogma, a set of beliefs and practices, which need constant reinforcement to compel compliance. So, revivals, appeals to the past, transient slogans such as "Make America Great Again," are efforts to revivify images and structures that have already lost their energy. Such belaboring of past values begets dictators of all stripes who sooner or later have to compel compliance because the resonance in the soul has long departed.

A few examples in the West will suffice: the death of Pan over two millennia ago produced "panic" in the Mediterranean cultures. Pan was the embodiment of agrarian and instinct-driven cultures that were being supplanted by the birth of the secular nation-states of Egypt, Persian, Greece, and Rome. In the third century of the Common Era, the collapse of the Roman order produced chaos and dismay. St. Augustine writes his *The City of God* to help believers counter the power of the secular order with the promise of an eternal kingdom beyond this world.

The pandemic of 1348-49 in Europe, killing approximately 40% of all communities, speeds the erosion of the claims for the divine right of royalty and religious institutions to impose absolutistic claims upon their residents. This erosion of mace and mitre led both to cultural ferment and the movement toward secular culture, with its urban clusters, polyglot communities, and cultures driven by commerce and secular values. I can continue to multiply the examples of such collective losses of meaning where the tribal picture no longer suffices to connect people in felt ways to the life of the spirit, or the longings of the soul.

Today, if a person were to ask, "Where is heaven?" as if there were a place, with an address and GPS fix, it would be seen as a naïve materialization of a psychospiritual query. There is no up—only "out there," for we now know this once center-of-the-universe planet is a speck of plasm tumbling through billions of galaxies. Few folks believe we started in 4004 B.C.E., when the evidence of radio telescopes, archeological evidence, geological data, and so on point to many millions of years of evolution. All in all, the position of the human ego has been greatly repositioned. Copernicus and others showed us we are a tiny part of those larger systems; Darwin demonstrated that the developmental process of the world continues, that we are not the apex of evolution but its current stage, with much more to come. And Freud and Jung demonstrated that we are not the rational creatures we thought but animals with cross-current agendas, reflexive responses to the world, and are pretty much unconscious most of the time. The string is untuned, as Shakespeare and his thoughtful colleagues in the 17th century began to intuit, leading to greater discordance within the collective myth and within individual souls.

However, there are many other signposts along the way. For example, we see in Kant's critique of traditional metaphysics—the effort to name and identify the nature of external reality—the necessity of modern psychology and phenomenology, which study the tools by which we construct our representations of reality. Additionally, traditional categories of belief—once thought to have derived from

Divine declaration, or in the nature of nature, such as gender roles and scripts, racial limits, moral values absolutistic in their claim, institutional stability and integrity—have been deconstructed and shown to be human constructs subject to prejudice, fear, complexes, and social constraints. The erosion of the fixed categories introduces an anxiety-generating ambiguity into the world but also frees the modern citizen to live a life of personal integrity and self-determination. Seemingly, only a few of our contemporaries are strong enough to accept this gift and the personal dignity and accountability it demands. Many still wish to fall back on old "certainties," fixed beliefs, or omnipresent distractions. It's easier that way than working things out for oneself.

Where to go then? With fundamentalisms of all kinds, militant and demanding, we see the triumph of anxiety over any emergent truth. With drugging pharmacopeias, inner conflict can be dissolved, and life fades into a cloud. With a wired, 24-hour pop culture, we see a treatment plan offering distraction and trivialization. Why any of us should care about the opinion of a celebrity with a big butt on some issue is beyond me. In the West, and much of the East, materialism, hedonism, and narcissism are the operative religions, no matter what a person might claim. What I should care about is what do *I* think and believe and choose? And even more than that, *why* I think, believe, and choose because the place from which these values come may not be a healthy, life-giving place, or may not be consonant with the wishes of the soul.

There are many communities of goodwill that serve their members through socialization and support. And many that frighten, or infantilize, or trivialize their members. It is important to know the difference. Many of them fail their adherents when things get really tough. But one can always ask a few basic questions: *Does the work of this group empower individuals to find their personal calling, live their personal journey, or does it wish to retain its members, preserve its status? Does the individual feel free to leave such a group without fear of sanction, judgment, or censure? Does the person grow, become a larger person through this affiliation, or does that person fold the summons of the personal journey into the collective ideology and the corporate group-think?*

All humans need to stand in relationship to something larger than their ego consciousness, something that reframes the ordinary experience of one day following another. In his memoir, *Memories, Dreams, Reflections*, Jung put this critical need this way. "Are we related to something infinite or not? That is the telling question of one's life. ... If we understand and feel that here in this life we already have a link with the infinite, desires and attitudes change. In the final analysis, we count for something only because of this essential we embody, and we do not embody that, life is wasted." *(MDR, p. 325.)*

Clearly, our modern treatment plans for what ails us—narcissism, distraction, trivialization, hedonism, materialism—do not work for us, or we would know it by now. And because our psyche is autonomous, it protests, throws up symptoms, makes us ill. Jung added that our neuroses, that is, inner splits, have to be understood as suffering that has not yet found its meaning. Thus, neurosis is the flight from "authentic" suffering. We do not escape this life without suffering, but our psyche demands that our suffering must matter. Those who live surfeited lives, full of distractions, diversions, abundance, still wake at 3 a.m. and stare into emptiness. What matters enough for us to suffer consciously? If we don't ask, and continue to ask that question, we will suffer, and not know why, or in service to what.

The chief suffering of our time occurs because most, not all, have lost connection to the numinous. When the supplicant brings this kind of suffering of the soul to the M.D. or the clergyman, Jung noted way back in 1931:

"The truth is, both doctor and clergy stand before him with empty hands…even when we see clearly why the patient is ill: when he sees that he has no love, only sexuality; no faith, because he is afraid to grope in the dark; no hope because he is disillusioned by the world and by life, and no understanding because he has failed to read the meaning of his own existence." {"Psychotherapy or the Clergy"}

The work of living between myths, between collective connectors to the numinous, is both a heavy weight of accountability, and a humbling process. And most of all, Jung adds, we have to confess our brokenness before any healing can begin. As he added:

"That I feed the beggar, that I forgive an insult, that I love my enemy…all these are undoubtedly great virtues. But what if I should discover that the least amongst them all, the poorest of all beggars, the most impudent of all offenders, yea the very fiend himself—that these are within me, and that I stand in need of the alms of my own kindness, that I am the enemy who must be loved—what then?" (*Ibid.*)

Without this confession of our spiritual poverty first, no healing, no larger story for us. Thus, the question that has to be addressed by all who wish to live consciously in the modern world is: *"By what values am I living my life, or what values are living me, without my consent, without my understanding?"*

A practical way of understanding this disconnect recognizes that the pursuit of "the latest shiny thing" will prove as successful and as satisfying as the last shiny thing(s). We have rather to ask: *What are our needs that are so little addressed by us that they have taken on such large proportions in the outer world, needs that we think we glimpse for a moment in the new shiny thing, and which now have become our pole star, our gyroscopes for navigating this journey?*

Our egoistic control towers are flush with discordant voices, and so we have to sort and sift and differentiate among those that come from outside, which ones from our disabling history, and which from our expectant soul. Even in the Bible, Jesus noted that one has to engage in a "testing of the spirits" to find which is which. One of the ways in which I have thought about this is:

If the numinous is not encountered within ourselves, our need for it will somaticize and damage the body, be distracted or anaesthetized by addiction, or will enter the world via projection onto objects of desire, which will then captivate and dominate us through their power.

****

So, how, then do we go about discerning more about our personal myth?

I think these questions may help you personalize this otherwise abstract concept. When we consider who we are and what we are doing, how often do we really probe *why* we are doing what we do? I may think I am performing a series of good acts, however defined by our time and place and level of awareness, but maybe they are simply conditioned behaviors. Sometimes they may be coming from codependent places or fear-driven places. When we challenge our deeper motives, we find rationalizations readily available to ratify, legitimize, perpetuate those behaviors. So, the first place to start probing what is going on in the unconscious begins here:

1. *What are your patterns?* Especially those you find counterproductive to you or possibly hurtful to others. Assuming that what we do is "rational, logical," based on the emotionally charged "story" inside us, what might that story be? When and where did you acquire that story? What is its message to you? Does it empower you in this world or diminish you? And what do you have to do to overthrow its sovereignty?

2. *Where are you stuck?* We all have stuck places, places where we know better, intend better, act better, but the same old, same old returns. What is that about? Why is it so easy to identify these roadblocks and so hard to get unstuck? If we choose to call something "stuck," then we imply that we imagine some behavior and attendant outcome that would be better.

What keeps us from that better behavior? The answer is always, always, *fear*. The moment we begin to move on the problem, our psychological history sends up immediate klaxon warnings: "beware, back off!" We may not hear those warnings, but our repetitive behavior tells us that we have succumbed to the system alert.

Only fear-based stories, or complexes, have the power to keep us stuck long after will and five-step plans have exercised their futile options. So, for example, the person who wants to stop smoking or overeating will have an abiding terror: "What will be there for me, what will connect me, what will soothe me, if not that?" And that's a very good question, and an important question. And it can only be answered by conscious addressing of that issue.

The stuck places are evidence of protections we learned early in our lives, sort of like surge protectors that shut down the excessive energy before it destroys your computer. We need to remember, always, that the inner machinery of the stuck places in our lives were put in place long ago and far away, most often in our early development. These protections—that is what they are and why they are so hard to transcend—derive from an early experience of our inadequacy in the face of the magnitude of the world around us. In those moments, we ignore that there is an adult, us, on the scene who is perfectly capable of managing those issues directly. They may not be easy, they may still be scary, but their engagement allows us to move into adulthood with the resources of a big person, finally.

3. *What are my avoidances?* The stuck places are avoidances, of course, but there are many more where we consciously avoid tense matters. Only sociopaths enjoy conflict. Most normal people don't. The question then is what is it I avoid and therefore undermine my value intentions? Let us say I don't speak up and let someone else's reality dominate the decisions. I may rationalize that as being amenable, but it is really rising

from the archaic precincts of fear. Where do I lack permission to really own my life? Where am I waiting for someone to give it to me? Do I want to be on the proverbial deathbed and be saying, "if only…?" Where do I need to be honest about my desires, my unspoken yearnings, curiosities, and inclinations? What will give me the momentum to step into my life while I am still here?

4. *What are my overcompensations?* By "overcompensation," we mean where do we work so hard to make something happen because our inner life is still so terrified if it does not? Why is it I am always trying to "fix" the other, mollify those upset, sacrifice my own well-being in service to bringing some homeostasis to the environment? (Remember the profile of "the wounded healer" in all us).

Given large experiences in our formation, and the large stories and defenses that arose in us from them, we have three choices: repeat them in our generation, run from them, or try to fix them in some way. If I look to my life choices, frequent strategies, is there a secret service working underground here? Is there some reactive repetition, flight, or reparation plan that I am enacting rather than living my life as if it were a different life, with a different destination than that of all the others? If I don't ask questions like this, one may be sure that one's life is being lived reactively rather than generatively. And one's psyche will not be amused.

5. *What are my symptoms?* What anxiety states perplex me; what depressions suck the joy out of my life; what "medications" am I employing to still the pain within?

Symptoms, remember, are psyche's way of getting our attention and indicating that the soul is not amused, that is, is wishing something better from us. So what if we are afraid and hiding out. When will we finally decide that now is the time to shut up, suit up, show up?

6. *What are your dreams telling you?* Jung said that dreams tell us the Tao of the moment—not what the ego thinks but what is really going on within us. If we live to 80, as I have been privileged to do, we will have spent six years of our lives dreaming, based on laboratory research into brainwave activity. That surely suggests that nature has some serious purpose in our dream life. Yes, it is true that our dreams help us process and metabolize the immense stimuli that flood us every day, but they also speak a mythological language. When asked why dreams are so difficult, more than clanking out telemessages to us to make one choice over another, Jung said, they bespeak an ancient language of nature that our culture has forgotten. So, as we sit with the metaphors and symbols that spontaneously rise in us each night, we begin to realize that they stir associations, sometime recognition, sometimes disquietude. In short, we are confronted with another intelligence within us. We can't disown that source because it is our dream, not an implant from someone else.

Over time, those who pay attention to their dreams—perhaps work with a therapist so trained, or not, and meditate, journal, reflect on whatever rises from below—begin to develop a deeper, more mature authority as opposed to succumbing to the messages we received from the world outside. Following our dreams is not only the *via regia* to the unconscious, as Freud claimed; it is also the descent into the shadow. But those nightly visitations are all meant in service to the soul and call upon us for healing, for balancing of life, and for growth and development.

There is something in all of us that won't let us get away with much. As my friend Stephen Dunn said in a poem about knowing himself pretty well, "that's the good news, and the bad news too." All depth psychological work is informative and humbling and challenging—no wonder so many of us avoid it.

 7. Living in *bonne foi*. Jean-Paul Sartre made much of living in *bonne foi* versus *mauvais foi*. Something in us always knows what is right for us even if the path toward it demands courage and persistence. Most of the time, we live in bad faith with ourselves and others, and at 3 a.m. know it. It is hard to hide then or scurry off.

When Jung said that neurosis is the flight from authentic suffering, he didn't spare us suffering. A life so oriented will prove fugitive and futile, superficial and sterile, as we so often observe in our world. The real question is: *What is worth your suffering*? If you run from that, you will experience a revolt from within, sooner or later. If you engage it, your life takes on richness. You are not flushed with happiness, which is transient in the best of times, but you are flooded with meaning. Meaning makes all things bearable. According to Camus in his *The Myth of Sisyphus*, even the hopelessness of Prometheus was replaced by the exercise of his choice to push that boulder up the hill, thus wresting from the gods themselves their terrible tyranny over him.

All our lives have such boulders from time to time, and we can run from them, deny them, but they wait for us in our sleep and in our unlived lives. Choosing them from time to time brings one into the presence of and the richness of the large. Our souls need to be in relationship to the large. As Rilke put it in one of his poems, our task is to "be defeated by ever-larger things." If we are engaging ever-larger things, then we are alive, growing, and in the midst of the dead all around, living our lives. The numinous, whether rising from below in us, or found in the opalescence of the world around us, leads us places where we were meant to go.

These seven suggested attitudes and practices help us move from identification with the internalized messages begun in childhood and carried through till today to a more authentic journey. Something inside each of us will always know the difference and will support us. We won't know that until we risk that. This commitment means leaving behind places of familiarity, zones of comfort and adaptation, and moving into the unknown. But when it is our journey, not the one imposed upon us, something always rises to guide us through. When Jung asserted that we all need to know what supports us when nothing supports us, he knew, and I have seen so many times, when we undertake the path we find is right for us, that path meant by the gods, we are never wholly alone, we are never without *resources,* and we are in the grip of something that cares for us, supports us.

The story is told of Admiral Richard Byrd explorations of the South Pole. On one occasion he was separated from his party and expected to perish. So, he wrote of his life and impending death in a logbook, hoping it would be found later. He was found, and when those notes were read later, many marveled at the equanimity with which he accepted his life and his death. This raises the question of what would be necessary for each of us to reach such a pinnacle of clarity and calm. I think two things: first, that we had lived our lives, and not someone else's, which is more difficult than it seems; and second, that we stood in the presence of something larger than we, and in so doing lived a larger life than our intimidations, our fears, our exempla from others, might have allowed. In that lifetime struggle, we will have found and served our personal myth, the one that brings us back to ourselves in a richer way, and the one that brings us to our appointments with the soul. Paradoxically, keeping that very personal appointment is how we bring something valuable to others as well.

Chapter Eleven

For Every Tatter in Our Mortal Dress:
Stayin' Alive at the Front of the Mortal Parade

An aged man is but a paltry thing,
A tattered coat upon a stick, unless
Soul clap its hands and sing, and louder sing
For every tatter in its mortal dress...

W. B. Yeats

Yeats wrote those words when he was aged, in physical pain, and sick at heart for the many disappointments in his life. No young person is allowed to write such words. One can only say, "Wait a few decades, see what life brings you, and then we will see...." Such a pronouncement may sound like cynicism, even bitterness, but it is not. It is simple realism. Let me cite five exemplary paradoxes of the problematics of aging in this troubled time between the gods, a time bereft of those larger rhythms of nature that enfolded individual journeys into a cosmic drama of redeeming inclusion.

1. In my academic youth, I was puzzled by a recurrent adage of Greek wisdom: "Best of all is not to have been born; second best is to have died young." Early in life I found this thought almost incomprehensible,

pessimistic, and antilife. Now I understand the wisdom, as well as the wry but futile hope of escaping life without its suffering. As Yeats elsewhere described the boundaries of our human condition: "man is in love, and loves what vanishes. / What more is there to say?" So, reader, is that ancient advice offered us cynical, bitter, or realistic? How does it measure up to the totality of our experiences? Are we able, willing, to embrace the ominous fullness of this life with all its festival of losses, which we otherwise desperately wish to prolong? If we live long enough, everyone we love will have died; if we don't, we will have left them. This is not pessimism; it is stale news.

2. A writer once interviewed me on the subject of the second half of life for a national periodical published by a major interest group and lobbyist for richer "senior living." She found her heuristic questions, and my responses, repeatedly edited and softened, irritatingly so. She got sufficiently heated as to finally visit the periodical's headquarters and confront the editors. She found, to her surprise and dismay, that most of them were in their 30s. How could they really understand what it means to be in one's 70s or 80s? No wonder their cover articles were mostly focused on "beautiful people" like Harry Belefonte and Faye Dunaway. They could not, understandably, imagine themselves other than in their present conditions and present state of minds.

3. In an earlier phase of professional life, when I was teaching undergraduates a course on the stages of life

development, I asked them to read the text with its quite illuminating examples and to write an essay imagining their lives two units or life cycles ahead of where they were. My silly thought was that perhaps knowing something of the road ahead might allow them to navigate its terrain a bit more consciously. How wrong I was. They read the material, which outlined the typical, even predictable issues and trials likely to arise for each stage, and they could accurately describe those issues, but when they came to imagining their lives in concrete settings or dilemmas similar to those described, they hit an imaginative wall, explaining how they and their wonderful partners, and their lovely, devoted children, adroitly sidestepped these pitfalls and moved to an ever-increasing domestic, professional, and philosophical bliss. This is one of the many reasons, and probably the most important, why I left college teaching in search of someone with whom to have a reality-based conversation. Yet the imaginative limits of these youth are rather common to us all. It is not the limit of intelligence or good intentions; it is the limitation of an experiential framework and a constricted imagination governed by complexes, wishes, and the seductive modes of denial to which we are all subject.

4. A number of years ago, I was invited to be a luncheon speaker at a "benefit" for the gerontology program of a nearby medical school. I went expecting to find an assembly of gerontology students and medical professionals. Instead, I found a group of impeccably

coifed, bedecked, bedizened, and bejeweled socialites. My talk addressed the greatest neurosis of our culture—the flight from aging and mortality, and its concomitant deification of longevity through phantasies of health, cosmetic and surgical beauty—and received the coolest smattering of applause. I apparently achieved a status as welcome in that beautiful assemblage of spring lime and tangerine finery as the ancient mariner with a dead bird around his neck. And how crazy must *I* be to say a disparaging word against longevity and health? (I am against neither, actually, but I did and do question *why* we should live longer, and in service to *what*, other than a narcissistic, timorous ego. And I did and do question why *more* of anything is somehow presumed superior to depth and purpose or the *why* of things). As a reminder to all of us, I did offer Jung's observation that "flight from life does not exempt us from the law of age and death. The neurotic who tries to wriggle out of the necessity of living wins nothing and only burdens himself with a constant foretaste of aging and dying, which must appear cruel on account of the total emptiness and meaninglessness of his life." (*CW5*, para. 617).

5. Adolph Güggenbuhl-Craig wrote a wonderful essay on "old age and fools" and did his best to disabuse us of any notion of "the golden years." He reminded that the body falls apart, friends and family die, and most plans and expectations crumble; however, one thing remains regnant: the power to act like a "fool" and get away

with it. After all, no one expects an aged person to be otherwise, especially in a youth-oriented, plastic, throw-away culture. Being a "fool" once again, the oxymoronic "wise fool," like the sopho-more (wise + moron), is an opportunity, Güggenbuhl-Craig argued, to recover an original psychological integrity, playfulness, and an unfettered desire for exuberant life.

So, what, then, given our cultural *Sitz-im-leben*, may I point to as a saving power for those who do not wish to go gentle into that good night, yet are not in denial of the nature of our nature, which is always naturing, always speeding us toward our mortal ends? Why should I—sharing a common condition of puzzlement over why we are here, what this life is about, and why we are apparently the only animal capable of reflecting upon its own dissolution and demise—have anything further to offer?

When the Dust Settles, With What Are We Left?

I do, however, have a modest assertion to leave with the reader. I believe as long as we are curious, we are still alive. The body will continue to decline according to the ministries of fate, lifestyle, genetics, and a host of unimaginably converging forces. Yet, Yeats was surely right. For every tatter in our mortal dress, soul must compensate. Bluntly put, for every outer decline, failure of powers, environmental constriction, *something within is challenged to grow apace.* Amid the wreckage of history, the carnage of loss, the growing catalog of grief, soul is summoned to grow.

I believe, even more today than before, that the quality of our lives will be a direct function of the magnitude of questions we ask, questions we are summoned to pursue for ourselves. And we do have to ask them on our own because there is precious little in our culture that does not elevate and privilege the banal, the distracting, the trivial—all of which are affronts and diminishments to the soul. (One celebrity type opined that she hoped that there was something after this life because if there wasn't, it would be oh so dreadfully boring).

Of course, the sanguinary sea-surge of aging and mortality are all the more troubling and unmediated for cultures that lose their mythic connections to the gods and to those great redeeming rhythms of death and rebirth of which we are such a tiny part. While our ancestors may have longed for a reunion in another world with their lost brethren or understood themselves an ineluctable part of a great cosmic cycle in which life and death are one—all a part of going home—most moderns experience their lives as fugitive egos, adrift, homeless, bereft, and disconnected from anything large or abiding.

In book after book and therapeutic hour after hour, I have asserted that the primary task of the so-called "second half of life" is the recovery of "personal authority." As children and young adults, we are obliged to adapt to the circumstances of family, time, place, zeitgeist, and the sundry vagaries of personal fate into which we are thrust. The so-called "first adulthood" is spent enacting or fleeing the messages we internalize from our phenomenological "reading" of life's text. One might summarize it this way: The agenda of the first half of life imposes adaptations of all kinds, and we all respond in our variegated ways to the demands, blows, challenges, and seductions of life, while the second half necessarily obliges sorting through the aftermath of choices and consequences: guilt, anger, recrimination, regret, recovery, and a summons to forgiveness of self and others. Thus, the second half of life is usually less a chronological event, a desperate resolve, than a persistently compelling subpoena to sort through that immense internal traffic we all carry and to discern what is true for us.

Many of us know, and many more of us suspect, there are no outer omniscient authorities anymore. The truth is, most of the people in positions of authority don't have a clue, and that is why they want, and need, the accoutrements of power. Accordingly, among the plethora of cacophonous claimants upon our values and choices, which ones are confirmed by our personal experience and which by our autonomous internal resonance? Then we are called to find the courage and consistency to live these truths in the world. Sounds easy, but it is truly a lifelong project. To facilitate this process in individuals, myself included, I have devoted the second half of my life in the venues of therapy, classrooms, and books to raise questions, challenge people to grow up, be accountable for these questions, and to work them through into more value-driven, rather than neurosis-driven, lives. (Jung pointed out that our private religions, the altars where we invest our most precious capital and spend most of our lives, is our daily service to our neuroses, namely, the "management systems" that temper our anxieties and solicit the satisfaction of our needs as best we can). To continue this assignment life apparently brings each of us, let me share some of those questions here.

In his eloquent *Letters to a Young Poet*, Rainer Maria Rilke advised that his reader be patient toward all that was unsolved in his heart. The task is always to live our answers with courage and fidelity. But, Rilke reminded, one is often not yet ready to live those answers. So, the task, he adds, is to live the questions faithfully until some distant day we live our way into our answers.

So it is, in the calculus of choice, *the larger the questions, the larger the journey we get!* As Arthur Mizner observed, it is doubt, not certainty, that gets us an education, and it is doubt and questioning that get us a more interesting life. Here are some questions which I think can, when lived with sincerity and personal integrity, lead to the enlargement of soul, even as the mortal tatters multiply.

Asking the Questions that Enlarge

"The meaning of my existence is that life has addressed a question to me … or conversely, I myself am a question." (Jung, *MDR*, p. 318)

1. *Where has fear blocked my development, kept me constricted, and still prevents me from risking who I am?* Anyone reading this book is now old enough, wise enough, to recognize, ruefully, that by and large we have been our own worst problem through the years. We are the only ones present in every scene of our long-running soap opera and

have reluctantly come to recognize that we often live in what Sartre called *mauvais foi*, or bad faith. Having acknowledged the necessity of adaptation, we grew defined by our strategies of conflict avoidance, sought the easier paths whenever possible, and surreptitiously transferred our dependencies to others: partners, organizations, ideologies. In our darkest hours, we admit to ourselves cowardice, dependencies, lies and deceptions, and other forms of slip-sliding away. We all know places where we failed to "show up." We are haunted by times when we let others down in service to our own narcissism or fugitive motives. No wonder old age can be so difficult. Physical pain and diminishment are nothing compared to rereading the catalog of personal shortcomings.

Well, the fat lady may be warming up just offstage, but it ain't over yet. As the noted American psychologist Yogi Berra said, "When you come to a fork in the road—take it!" Ask yourself where fear still blocks you. Having asked that question, whatever comes up on your personal screen is your new agenda. This does not mean that you have to take up skydiving, or sell all and move to a monastery, though either might be right for a person here or there. It means that you decide that honesty with the world begins with honesty with yourself. It then means speaking truthfully with others rather than avoiding. It means following that curiosity which lies at the heart of human nature wherever your physical and imaginative powers permit you to travel. In some cases, this will mean recovering the interest, the talent, the enthusiasm left behind. In other cases, it will mean risking doing what you wish to do with your precious time and energy whether it fits in with others, whether approved by others, and whether difficult or not. If we can hold to what is difficult to us, we will find that we are serving life, not death, growth, not aversive adaptation. And if not now, when?

2. *What unlived life of my parents am I still carrying and passing on to my descendants?*

Jung's comment that the greatest burden of every child is the unlived life of the parents surely haunts all of us. In the face of a powerful outer exemplum, such as the parent/child dynamic, our most common tendency is to serve its message. Thus, we may be blocked where our parents were blocked— in emotional freedom, in the capacity for risk, in affirming our sexuality, our personal passions, our enthusiasms. Or, secondly, we will have spent our life in compensation for the shortfalls of the other. So, in saying we will not be like our mothers or not live our father's life, we are still being defined by that other, rather than from the natural source within us all. Or, thirdly, we will have devoted, and may still devote, our lives to an unconscious "treatment" plan, such as an addiction to numb the cleavage within ourselves, or a life of frenetic busyness, or a life of distraction. (Our contemporary popular culture offers unparalleled distractions. People can stay wired, tuned in, numbed 24 hours a day, and more and more of us are doing precisely that. Someday soon we will be dead, and how will we have spent these last years, these last hours)?

In addition, our internal blockages are passed on to our children, our descendants, and constitutes a signal burden to them as well. We say we love our children, but are we sparing them the need to take care of our emotional lives? Are we dumping our unrequited needs upon them? Are we living through them, or their children—our presumptive, redemptive simulacrums? And will our descendants, as a result, breathe a secret sigh of relief when they no longer have to carry us?

And have we forgotten that they all are, even the estranged ones, still looking to us to provide the model, the mentoring? How we deal with our aging, our impending death, our physical limitations, our losses, disappointments, and difficult hours are lessons they are absorbing day by day. With what courage, or lack thereof, do we face our difficult and narrowing journey, with what immaturity and neediness do we defer to others, with what wisdom do we embody or fail to address are they absorbing every day, whether we know it or not, and whether they now know it or not.

If we have lived small questions, and therefore small lives, they will too, or be forced to compensate for the life we shunned. If we did not step into our summons to grow up, how or why would we ever expect them to?

3. *What, really, is my spirituality, and does it make me larger or smaller?*

For many, the word *spirituality* is loaded with painful, regressive associations of religious dogma shoved down their throats, guilt complexes, and fear-based agendas. Yet, *spirit* remains the best word we have to describe that quickening of the soul and body that is the spark of life. What animates us, what drives us forward into life? That is to say, our spirituality is not what we say it is, but where we in fact invest our energies on a daily basis. Such investments are the true standard and only measure of our spiritual values.

How many of us can pass Freud's elemental test of spirituality? He noted over a century ago that most folks fill the immensity of the mystery of our cosmos with jury-rigged theologies that replicate parental complexes, assuage the terrible uncertainties of life with shaky assurances, and, surprise, adopt theologies and practices that ratify our neuroses or serve comforting narcissistic agendas. Our gods, in other words, sound surprisingly like us. How many of us can maturely examine our *imago Dei*, and we all have one, whether conscious or not, and query whether it leads us deeper us into life and its unfathomable mysteries or helps us avoid the wonder and terror of uncertainty and mystery? How much mystery can we tolerate? How much ambiguity?

Such questions are not really about the mysteries of our universe; they are about us, about our personal psychologies, and our relative psychological maturity. Until we recognize that our theologies and spiritual practices speak mostly about us, Rorschach confessions in effect, then we will remain encased less in a spiritual respect for the mystery than in a shabby avoidance of it. The purpose of a mature spirituality is to live in depth, whether in the venues of loss and uncertainty or those of plentitude.

A mature spirituality is one that allows the old images to go because they were only that—*images*. The image is not the mystery. The mystery is the energy that informs the universe, that once animated those images, and that still courses through us. It is natural for ego consciousness to grab hold of the image, to fasten on to it in service to our various security agendas. But that energy will not be contained in the image or our subsequent understandings and practices. By the time we have "fixed" the mystery, it is already gone. During my "individuation" exam in Zürich's Jung-Institut many years ago, one of the examiners said, solemnly, "My individuation began the day my God died." We all knew what she meant. Her *imago Dei* was no longer charged with energy, no longer numinous, and then she knew she had to grow up and take on the responsibility for the conduct of her journey.

The proper summons to ordinary consciousness then, is not to cling to what is already gone, but to abide the in-between, to embrace the wonder of the uncertain, and to remain open to the next venue in which the mystery might manifest. Sounds easy enough, but it is difficult to be strong enough to be that vulnerable. And yet, the energies of the universe will as they may and shall pay no attention whatsoever to what we expect of them.

The most religious statement I have heard on this matter is Jung's confession that he called *God* that which crossed his willful path and altered his conscious intentions for good or for ill. In other words, whatever radically reframes the ego's sense of self and world, whatever obliges us to come in naked humility before the Other anew, is a spiritual encounter. So, beware, then, of seeking religious experience. One might in fact get one. (Is this why so many religious institutions and practices protect one from religious encounter and thereby ensure a diminishing, fear-driven, avoidant journey)?

Notice how respectful of mystery Jung's concept is. Notice how it does not pander to fear or manipulate the concepts to fit personal needs. Notice how it passes Freud's test by enlarging beyond narcissistic self-interest and neurosis management to encounter the radical, intractable "otherness" of the universe. Such an openness, such a relinquishment of our puny power agendas, may in fact prove worthy of the word *spirituality*. It will ask of us so much more than that of which we are comfortable. It will ask of us that we confess our smallness in the face of the largeness of the mystery, but that is the only way we can really respect the mystery and its sovereign autonomy. Such a confession, while challenging the fear-based, inflated ego, is in fact already a spiritual enlargement.

4. *Where do you refuse to grow up, wait for clarity before risking, hope for external solutions, expect rescue from someone, or wait for someone to tell you what your life is about?*

This last is a particularly loaded question, a charged query, and yet never have I had anyone ask me in the context of a workshop, "What do you mean," and never has anyone paused long before journaling in a personal response to these questions. Such a response tells me that we all "know" and that we suffer both that "knowing" and the stuckness that so often attends. If we really "know," why would we remain stuck? Well, the answer is now clear: *It is not about what it is about.* That is to say, the "stuckness" is not about the particular issue we confront, or which confronts us, it is about how a "circuitry" from that resistant locus reaches down to an earlier, recalcitrant place, an archaic zone in our psyches that, when activated, floods us with anxiety, whether we know it or not. Swimming in such discomfort, we naturally prefer stuckness to going through such discomfort as is required to get to the other side.

These questions all evoke "shadow" aspects of our psychic life—namely, the encounter with that which threatens ego stability and security, seems contrary to our values, or asks more of us than we figure we can imagine. Thus, we privilege the *status quo ante* and indict ourselves at the same time for so electing stuckness. We hate being "stuck," but we hate dealing with the discomfiture getting unstuck will require even more.

When we unpack the clauses above one by one, we see that "growing up" means not only being conscious but being accountable for doing something about what consciousness brings to us. Imagine that! Growing up would mean that we are out there on our own and tremendously vulnerable. Yet, we learned so long ago to adapt, avoid, rationalize, and precisely to arm ourselves against such exposure. This archaic defense mechanism has brought us this far, so we fear stirring up those lower powers if we can avoid them, even now fleeing in the face of accumulated consequences and troubling dreams.

The timorous ego naturally prefers clarity, certainty, the illusion of control, and will even distort reality in order to provisionally obtain it, as we may surmise from the slippery spiritualities described above. Yet, life is a risk. Even as we admire those who historically set out upon susurrant seas, filled with monsters of seduction and devouring appetites, we all find it safer to hug the shore, safer to wait for certainty—a certainty that will never come—till the day someone pounds that last nail in our coffin.

In hoping for external solutions, we perpetuate our infantile dependency on parents or, far more subtly, parental surrogates. We may conduct the most responsible, productive outer lives, when measured against the materialist metrics of our meretricious times, and yet defer the summons to personal authority and the isolation and courage that requires. Simply to remind ourselves, personal authority means sorting through the immensity of inner and outer traffic, to "test the spirits" as the *Book of John 4:1* has it, and finding what is true for us, experientially and intuitively validated, and then the courage to live it in the world.

Similarly, the frightened, isolated child within each of us is still looking for someone to take care of us. Fortunately, that person has finally arrived, long after we futilely sought such a person in our partners, our institutions, our ideologies. That person is us. Better get used to trusting them, for they are the best we have, and will ever get.

So often we look for someone else to explain life to us: a preacher, a politician, a friend, a parent, a therapist, an institution, a creed, a tradition. While all may be useful in partial ways, no one source will provide us with sufficient insight into this complexly changing world and to the incredibly labyrinthine layers of our own psyche. Besides, what is true for another, however sincerely transmitted, will seldom prove adequate to us. We cannot have someone else live our lives for us, though many parents try. We cannot ask others what our life is about because they seldom have made much headway on figuring out their journey, let alone ours. (This does not mean that there are not many, many people out there perfectly willing to tell you how to live your life. I do not count myself among them. As a teacher/therapist, my job is to listen, offer ideas, examples, and so on, but most of all, to ask you to figure it out for yourself and then live what you find into the world). And whatever you figure out for today will not apply a few years down the line, so better plan on going back to the drawing board from time to time.

Your ego will not like this uncertainty, but in the end, it will not have a choice. Surely, this is what Jung meant in his memoir, *Memories, Dreams, Reflections,* when he said that life has addressed a question to him, and that he himself is a question. What questions has life asked of you? What have you had to struggle with, to overcome, to understand? We may complain about what life gave us, but the meaning of all of our journeys persists: How much of yourself were you able to claim, to embody in the world in the face of the obstacles fate presented you? Where are you challenged to grow beyond your comfort zone? What "question" are you embodying? Your individuation process is your "answer," so might we decide that it shall be the best we can provide.

Staying Alive

In 1978, I had finished my first year of studies in Zürich and was returning with family to Luxemburg to catch the then-budget *Loftleider* flight back to the U.S. via Iceland. En route, while staying in a youth hostel in Paris, we heard the Bee Gees sing "Staying Alive" for the first time. My spirit was lifted, and I am lifted every time I hear it still. I think the appeal of that disco song is not the eponymous theme of perpetuating this ego. Rather, it quickens the spirit in its jaunty, in-your-face rhythm. It has, as they say in Philly, attytood! So, the spirit is found in the attytood we bring to this miserable, wondrous, brief transit called life.

It is the troubling conundrum of our condition that the alternative to aging and dying is called "early death." It is perplexing and paradoxical to the ego state that we are forever speeding toward our own temporal dissolution. Accordingly, we have created sundry drugs, ideologies, and distractions to finesse this reality, but all of them are not the friend but the enemy of life. Plato observed nearly three millennia ago that the well-lived life demands the daily contemplation of death. He was not being morbid; that we might think so is rather the morbidity of our neurosis—our rejection of the gift of this paradox-driven life. Plato is rather asking for a more thoughtful journey, a more solemn, considered, value-driven, and dignified conduct of this precious, precarious life. As for death, it will come soon enough. Essentially, whatever we think about that telluric *telos* is essentially irrelevant. Either this ego consciousness is obliterated, rendering all speculation, anxiety, and hope moot, or it is a transformation so beyond our imaginative powers that we cannot fathom its possibilities. All that will take care of itself. Meanwhile, the task is to live.

In the face of progressive physical diminishment, what we have as our continuing companion faculties are our imagination and our curiosity. As long as they are present, we are alive, and growing, and developing. Meanwhile, might we manage to stop whining and kvetching? As G. B. Shaw put it, let us affirm "being a force of nature instead of a feverish clod of ailments and grievances complaining that the world will not devote itself to making [us] happy." Let us risk letting go of our fearful, tenuous grip on life whereby, ironically, we remain enslaved to the fear of death. Let us embrace dying unto our previous life, and the fear that keeps us from the new, lest we die before we die. As Goethe put it,

> ...so long as you haven't experienced
> This: to die and so to grow,
> You are only a troubled guest
> On the dark earth.

Afterword

This journey we call our life began long before we began, for all of us are carrying our ancestral, cultural, and genetic histories. The findings of epigenetics reveal to us that even the traumas of our ancestors can affect our neural pathways, our proclivities to certain disorders, and even our length of life, as studies of subsequent generations of Holocaust survivors and U. S. Civil War wounded prisoners of war have revealed. So, apparently, we are launched in certain directions before we breathe that first breath.

Initially floating through a timeless fluid, then, after a series of convulsive shocks, we are flung into this world: tiny, vulnerable, and utterly at the mercy of fate in our traumatic deposition into time and space. None of us reading these words would be here without the fortuity of someone sacrificing selfish interests to protect, feed, and clothe us. What a stunning achievement it is that any of us survive.

Within that neonate, two energies contend, and will always contend—the regressive urge to fall back into that "Edenic," conflict-free state, and the progressive urge to move forward, to grow and to develop. Every day these forces contend. One serves the profound desire to "go Home," where the gain is quiescence amid life's tumult, and one serves development where the price is struggle and heartbreak. Historically, humans have found supportive measures for each of these motives. For the regressive tendency: comforting ideologies that lull one to sleep through denial and arbitrary "certainty," drugs and alcohol, and the capacity to remain immature, to flee the accountability adulthood requires of us. Historically, to serve the progressive tendency: rites of passage that mobilize libido in service to developing a mature vision and capacity, exemplary stories of heroism and achievement to inspire, and the respect of others that arises from the journey fully taken were present to help souls on their way. In his 1912 book *Symbols of Transformation*, Jung noted that, on the one hand, we awaken each day to a deadly longing for the abyss, to fall back into the sleep of childhood; and on the other hand, nature provides each of us with the archetypal "hero" energy whose task it is to serve life and overthrow the powers of darkness when they come to us in forms of fear and intimidation, or the seductions of denial and flight.

Every day, then, this fierce struggle transpires in each of us. Every day, the fate of the world, the needs of the future, and the unfolding of nature or Divinity's possible expressions are up for grabs in each of us. Every day. It never ends. No matter what we did yesterday, or failed to do, the invitation, the challenge, the tormenting tension of opposites return today.

****

As I look over this collection of essays, written recently, and over the past decade, a central theme leaps out at me. This book is called *Prisms* because when I was in fifth grade, our teacher brought several glass pyramids into our classroom to enjoy before and after class. Meant originally for the periscopes in submarines and tanks in World War II, we loved how those chunks of glass distorted the world, just as we loved running into each other or the walls. But even then, this refractory dissonance caused me to reflect on what is reality and how do we implicate ourselves in its construction? If the world I was seeing through the glass was not as it was, could it be such is the case other times too? I don't recall how I languaged that at the time—I was 10, but I do recall wondering this. So, without knowing it, I had tumbled to the need for phenomenology and depth psychology, but it would be decades before I knew that others had had the same questions and had worked to find ways to address them.

So, whatever our prisms, they distort the Other always. Our eyes, our psychologies, our tribal affiliations—all distort the other. So much bloodshed, persecution, bigotry, and sorrow has come from folks assuming that what they see in the other is what they really are. They are not yet aware of projections and how whatever is unconscious in any of us tends to leave us and fall upon the other as an interpretation, a reading, a defining brief.

So, if I am afraid of the otherness of the world, even the otherness in me, why would I not also be afraid of you, grow defended, perhaps hostile toward you? This fear of the other has generated the lamentable catalog of human suffering. Remembering that most of our ancestors lived in tribal units of 50 to 200, we realize their survival may well have depended on this vigilance. But we, with our lethal weapons, exposed to common problems, destroying the air around us, drowning in viral pathogens, can we afford that suspiciousness, that paranoia anymore?

Each of these essays you have read rose from an effort to understand, to see what was coursing beneath the surface, and to offer some perspective upon it, even if it was only my distorted perspective as seen through my prism. Just as Plato argued that the task of philosophy is to tell those chained in the cave of unconsciousness that the shadows against the back wall that they see are not the reality, so the work of depth psychology seeks to help us examine the stories, the distortions, the splinter narratives that otherwise direct our lives. How, in this mélange of images, in this existential limitation we call the human condition, can we know anything? Good question. All we can do is continue to inquire, to be aware of the limits of our knowledge, to resist seduction by the insistent voices of our society, and the noisome chatter of our complexes. All we can do is confess our ignorance, which, as Socrates concluded so long ago, is the beginning of wisdom. To know we don't know, to understand that we must not presume, to track the movements of all things, outer and inner, and ask *where do they come from, really,* and *what do they serve,* is to engage the vertiginous mystery that informs us all and in which we swim as ignorant fish. From that committed inquiry, we get more and more puzzles, more and more growth, and more to share with others. Most of all, from that we get a more interesting life, and that is as good as it gets. Not certainty, friends, rather, *a more interesting life!* Just be glad you have been here, witnessed so much stuff, good and bad, and do appreciate that so much more is to come.

And as for me, as I near the end of my journey, I am so deeply grateful for those who loved me beyond any merit of mine—that is called "grace," so my life has been graced. There are many faces passing before me as I think on my gratitude. I am grateful for those who taught me things, helped me build a never-ending school from the timbers I received, and so in thanks I have devoted my entire adult life to the teaching profession. That service was never a sacrifice; it was always the right thing for me to do, the serving of my personal myth. For those times when I made choices that hurt me or others I am profoundly sad and can only ask their forgiveness even as I find forgiving myself the hardest of all things to do. (While reminded daily of my shortcomings, I never felt superior to anyone else. We need to remember that the etymology of *condescension* means "we all fall together"). As long as the journey continues, there is so much more to learn, and therefore so much more to live and to share. The schoolhouse keeps getting larger, the prisms more and more complex, and so this journey grows more and more interesting.

Bibliography

Camus, Albert. *The Myth of Sisyphus*. New York: Vintage, 2018.

Dostoevski, Fyodor. *Notes from Underground*. New York: New American Library, 1961.

Ellmann, Richard: *Yeats: The Man and the Masks*. New York: E. P. Dutton and Co., 1948.

Frost, Robert. "For Once, Then, Something," http://www. poetryfoundation.org/poem/173528

von Goethe, Johann, "The Holy Longing," in Robert Bly, James Hillman, and Michael Meade, eds. *The Rag and Bone Shop of the Heart: Poems for Men*. New York: Harper, 1993.

Hollis, James. "Convergent Patterns in Yeats and Jung," *Psychologic Perspectives*: Vol. 4, Issue 1, pp. 60-68, 1973, and Vol. 48, Issue 2, pp. 288-297, 2006.

_____. *Living Between Worlds: Finding Personal Resilience in Changing Times*. Boulder, CO: Sounds True, 2020.

_____. (1995) *Tracking the Gods: The Place of Myth in Modern Life*. Toronto: Inner City Books.

_____. (1996) *Swamplands of the Soul: New Life in Dismal Places*. Toronto: Inner City Books.

_____. (2007) *Why Good People Do Bad Things: Understanding our Darker Selves*. New York: Gotham/ Penguin.

Jung, Carl. *The Collected Works of C. G. Jung.* Ed. H. Read, Michael Fordham, G. Adler, and Wm. McGuire. Princeton: Princeton University Press, 1953-79. [abbreviated *CW* in this book.]

_____. *Memories, Dreams, Reflections*. Ed. Aniela Jaffé. New York: Pantheon Books, 1961. (abbreviated *MDR* in this book).

_____. (2007) *The Jung-White Letters*. London: Routledge.

MacLeish, Archibald. *J.B.: A Play in Verse*. New York: Houghton-Mifflin, 1968.

Martel, Yann. *The Life of Pi*. New York: Mariner Books, 2003.

Menninger, Karl. (1988) *Whatever Became of Sin?* New York: Bantam.

Pascal, Blaise. *Pensees*. New York: Penguin Classics, 1995.

Rosenbloom, Ron. *Explaining Hitler: the Search for the Origin of His Evil*. New York: Harper, 1999.

Thomas, Camaron J. *The Wisdom of the Brain: Neuroscience for Helping Professions*. North Charleston, SC: Create Space, 2016.

Yeats, William Butler. *The Collected Poems of W. B. Yeats*. New York: The Macmillan Company, 1963.